THE DEVELOPING COUNTRIES

Employment and Capital Investment

S. A. KUZ'MIN

Editor, English-Language Edition
LEONARD J. KIRSCH

Routledge
Taylor & Francis Group

LONDON AND NEW YORK

The Developing Countries
Employment and Capital Investment

First published 1969 by International Arts and Sciences Press, Inc.

Reissued 2018 by Routledge
2 Park Square, Milton Park, Abingdon, Oxon OX14 4RN
711 Third Avenue, New York, NY 10017, USA

Routledge is an imprint of the Taylor & Francis Group, an informa business

A Library of Congress record exists under LC control number: 68014669

ISBN 13: 978-1-138-04540-8 (hbk)
ISBN 13: 978-1-138-04545-3 (pbk)
ISBN 13: 978-1-315-17193-7 (ebk)

Contents

Introduction

One of the most important and urgent economic problems confronting the developing countries of Asia, Africa, and Latin America is that of industrialization. While the economic history of presently developed capitalist countries demonstrates various approaches to the solution of this problem, none of them can be regarded as a ready recipe for the young sovereign nations that are struggling for total independence.

The most important specific feature in the present economic situation of the developing countries is that, as a result of the colonial and imperialist exploitation of many years, the majority of them have a national economy that is exhausted and devastated. Their initial accumulation reserves have been systematically drained off into the developed capitalist countries. A backward, one-sided economy, unchanging agriculture, a very weak industry, and an undeveloped, disorganized credit system are unable to provide the resources that are essential for rapid industrial development. Accordingly, the problem of resources — very important to any country entering the stage of industrialization — is extremely acute for the developing nations.

Exhausted by colonial exactions, the national economy of economically underdeveloped countries has developed at a slower pace than their population growth. Consequently, with each passing year it has been increasingly difficult to maintain even a minimum level of consumption. It would be no exaggeration to say that in the postwar period, a number of colonies and dependent countries were faced with economic catastrophe. At the present time, the economic situation in these countries, the majority of which have won national independence, continues to be strained. From this arises another problem — specifically, the problem of the economic growth rate.

At the present time there are a number of factors that facilitate and reduce the time necessary for the creation of an independent and flourishing economy in the developing countries. The most important among these is the fact that in their struggle for political and economic independence, the developing countries are not isolated but rather enjoy the moral and growing material support of the socialist countries. By using the experience of the world socialist economic system in the practical solution of basic socioeconomic problems, they are able to accelerate their own development. Both the specific difficulties of the developing countries, resulting from their dependent position of long standing, and the factors favoring the formation of these countries cannot but find expression in economic policies, in their selection of one or another solution of national economic problems.

The basis for the industrialization of the developing countries has been and continues to be the creation of their own production of the means of production on the basis of modern science and technology. Without their own sufficiently developed production of the means of production they will continue to be in the position of a "world village." Even the emergence of certain raw materials processing branches in these countries will not change this situation, because the dependence of their economy on the industrially developed capitalist countries will not only not diminish but in a number of cases will increase. Only the development of the key branches of industry can serve to lessen this dependence and promote a basic reorganization of the colonial structure of the economic systems of these countries.

Unquestionably, in the creation of the leading branches of the national economy, the developing countries must make use of more modern and therefore more productive technology because only the application of such technology can place their production in terms of profitability on a par with production in the developed countries. However, several points on this basic principle require clarification.

First, in no way does the principle of the necessity for the developing countries to create their own production of the means of production imply an appeal for an "isolated" economy. In order to make use of the advantages of international exchange, the developing countries must stand more firmly on their own feet and reduce their dependence on the world market in providing the vital needs of reproduction. This is precisely the end that is served by the production of the most essential elements of social capital.

Second, this basic principle does not apply equally to all developing countries because there are great differences in the level of economic development, in the supply of raw materials and other resources for the creation of heavy industry, and in the capacity of the internal market. For example, while such countries as India, Pakistan, the UAR, Indonesia, and certain others can in full measure and with advantage for themselves develop the production of the means of production, in a number of other countries this may prove unadvisable at the present stage. This may be the case for the majority of nations on the African Continent for which, to all appearances, it would be most advantageous to create production of the means of production within an entire region or several regions.

The process of industrialization in the developing countries is inseparably linked to profound social and economic transformations, in particular to a change in the existing agrarian relations, to the elimination of the dominance of moneylenders in agriculture and in handicraft work, to restrictions on the activities of large-scale national capital, to the liquidation of the predominance of foreign monopolies in the most important spheres of the national economy, to the democratization of social life, etc. Undoubtedly, industrialization will only be successful in these countries if technical and social progress go hand in hand. For the developing countries, with their agricultural and raw material specialization, the problem of industrialization means not only the creation of the key branches of industry but also the radical reorganization of the entire economy as a whole and profound changes in the very structure of the economy. Each leading branch of industry must be supplied with materials on the basis of domestic production. Otherwise, a lessening of dependence on the world market for some types of commodities will be offset by the intensification of this dependence for other types of commodities. Accordingly, in these nations, industrialization means the development of a complex of production facilities, a complex which, while sufficiently broad, is not necessarily all-encompassing. The development of branches in Department I must be accompanied by corresponding development of branches in Department II; in turn, each basic branch in both Departments must develop in close contact with production facilities preparing raw materials and semifinished goods for it, and providing it with spare parts, repairs, etc.

This kind of comprehensiveness in the development of industry in countries entering the stage of industrialization presupposes a special multivariant solution of their economic problems. One of the most important problems of this type is the distribution of capital among various national economic branches. The majority of developing countries do not have the possibility of developing an entire industrial complex at once and are forced to do this consecutively, in several stages. This presupposes the existence of several variants for channeling priority investments. The selection of an optimal variant is possible only on the basis of the scientific analysis of interbranch relationships and the construction of a dynamic model. Another problem is the intrabranch distribution of capital investments — in other words, the selection of the best mode of production of one and the same product. The discovery of an optimal solution to this problem is especially urgent for the developing countries.

Even though the economic situation of various developing countries is far from uniform, nonetheless, a large group of these countries has a number of common features. In studying the economies of the majority of countries in Asia and a number of countries in Africa and Latin America, the first thing that becomes apparent is the existence of immense and, to a considerable extent, unused human resources as well as an acute shortage of productive capital. To a large extent, the insufficient rate and dimension of capital accumulation are explained by social and economic conditions in developing countries: the increasing concentration of social wealth in the hands of privileged classes; the dominance of moneylenders and numerous commercial middlemen in all basic spheres of economic life; the continuing exploitation of these countries on the part of foreign monopolies, etc. All these factors are based on the colonial and imperialist exploitation of these nations for many years and on the resulting impoverishment of the very base of primitive capital accumulation.

The present dimensions of accumulation in these countries do not permit the employment of the growing able-bodied population, especially if the resources are expended solely on the creation of enterprises of the modern type, i.e., highly mechanized enterprises. The employment problem confronts economists — theoretical and practical — in developing countries with the serious task of finding such a combination of various forms of production as would permit the optimal use of both the sparse financial resources and the mass of manpower, which is "redundant" under present conditions. Unques-

tionably, the solution must be maximally effective and must most completely correspond to the interests of the national economy as a whole; at the same time it must employ the largest number of able-bodied workers. In this sense, of very great importance is the use of forms of production that differ in the amount of productive capital per worker (henceforth this concept will be termed "capital-intensiveness"). There are many such forms of production, or technological modes, especially in the developing countries where modern highly productive and correspondingly quite capital-intensive forms of production go hand in hand with less capital-intensive and less productive forms all the way to mass manual labor.

Two large groups of industrial enterprises that differ most with respect to capital-intensiveness — factory and small-scale (1) production — have been taken as the subject of the present investigation. Of course, it is impossible to draw a precise boundary between these two groups. Frequently it is difficult to say where small-scale production ends and factory production begins. The official statistics of developing countries resorts to a purely conditional division (most frequently in terms of the number of persons employed) of industrial enterprises into factory (those "qualifying" for inclusion in this group) and small-scale, handicraft enterprises. Inasmuch as we do not have any other statistics at our disposal, however, we shall have to use this unquestionably somewhat simplified classification.

Owing to inadequacies in the statistical information, a number of enterprises having the features of one group fall into another, and vice versa. For example, a number of small-scale enterprises having modern equipment and characterized by capital-intensiveness and labor productivity on a par with that of the "large-scale" enterprises may, on the basis of employment, fall into the same catagory with individual handicraft workers and workshops based on manual labor. And, on the other hand, on the same basis — the number of workers — a number of large manufacturers [manufaktury — used in the Marxist historical sense, basically manual labor] may be included in the factory industry. To a greater or lesser extent, errors of this type inevitably slur over the most characteristic features both of factory and of small-scale production. Nonetheless, there is a possibility (and the statistical materials cited below confirm this) of isolating certain of the most important features in both forms of production, which must be differentiated in the process of planning the development of these two types of production.

The basic features of small-scale industry are as follows: (2)

(1) the relatively small number of persons employed, even though, as noted above, the boundary between small-scale industry and factory industry in this respect is very conditional;

(2) the limited size of the fixed capital used (it is supposed that the capital of a small-scale enterprise does not permit it to use modern, highly productive equipment accessible only to a factory);

(3) the use of "unpaid" labor by members of the family side by side with hired labor (the owner of the enterprise for the most part participates in the production process personally);

(4) the extensive use or even the predominance of manual labor over mechanized labor (of course, the possibility of the partial use of mechanical energy is not excluded). On the whole, small-scale industry can be defined as production with a low level of mechanization as opposed to highly mechanized modern forms of industrial production, which are united under the term "factory industry."

As will be shown below, the existence of the aforementioned common features of small-scale production does not preclude the entry into small-scale production of forms that are very different in their social significance. Village handicraft still continues to be a widespread form of small-scale production in the majority of developing countries. The village handicrafts-man works for a specific customer, i.e., he chiefly serves the needs of his fellow villagers (black-smith work, cabinetmaking and carpentry, pottery, etc.). In this aspect, village handicrafts still bear many features of the natural [natural'-noe] economy and are the most stable precisely in the most remote regions, far from the capitalist market. As commodity-monetary relations develop, village handicraft workers also become involved in the process of commodity production and, in addition to working on orders, they manufacture goods for an unknown consumer and sell them at the nearest market. As a rule, village handicraft goods are of low quality and cannot compete with inexpensive factory goods. On the whole, village handicrafts combine features of natural and small-scale commodity production.

In the developing countries, the existence of large rural regions almost untouched by "civilization" maintains a great significance for this form of industrial production. More than upon direct actions by the government, the prospect for the development of village handicrafts to a greater extent depends upon the development of the economy of these countries as a whole and of the so-called backward regions in particular, the growth of modern industry, the construction of means of communication, etc.

Various types of small-scale urban industry may be of considerable interest in the elaboration of the government's industrial policy. A large group in small-scale urban production is constituted by numerous types of production in the home. These forms include the following: the craftsman who still owns the implements and means of production and has at least formal independence, the handicraft worker who has been partially expropriated by merchant-money-lender capital, and the small-scale commodity producer who has essentially already become a hired worker and who works on the orders of others and with the tools of others but still works at home (dispersed manufactures). The latter form of production at home is particularly widespread in the developing countries of Asia.

Another important type of small-scale production is the manufacture, which differs greatly in dimensions. As already noted above, some manufacture types are so large that, in terms of the number of persons employed, they fall into the group of factory enterprises. Nonetheless, relatively small enterprises predominate. As a rule, the modern manufacture in the developing countries is partially outfitted with mechanical machine tools (usually obsolescent), but manual labor is predominant. Like craft work at home, the manufacture depends greatly on merchant-moneylender capital. Under small-scale industry we can also classify such enterprises (small factories) in which the majority of the operations are performed mechanically; here, however, the enterprise is outfitted with obsolescent low-productivity equipment. With respect to labor productivity, the gap between these enterprises and factory industry is so great that for convenience of analysis and practical planning it is advisable to classify them as a part of the group of small enterprises.

What is the socioeconomic essence of present-day small-scale urban production? On the one hand, it continues to retain the basic traits of small-scale commodity production, traits characterizing industry in the manufacture stage — specifically, the predominance of manual labor and simple cooperation, the sporadic use of machines, the relatively small volume of production and market, etc. (3) Even though it is not always necessarily the case, a very widespread feature in small-scale production is the personal participation of the owner of the means of production and members of his family in the production process. This holds true not only for craft work in the home but also for the manufacture and even the small factory. All these factors place the small commodity producer in a special stratum of the urban petty bourgeoisie. At the same time, under the conditions of a dominant capitalist structure, small-scale production becomes one of the forms of capitalist production, and the craftsman, even though he does not resort to hired labor, is a capitalist in a certain sense.

Characterizing the position of the craftsman under capitalism, Marx noted: "In the capacity of owner of the means of production he is a capitalist. In the capacity of a worker he is his own hired worker. Thus, as a capitalist, he pays himself wages and extracts profit from his capital, i.e., he exploits himself as a hired worker and, in the form of surplus value, pays himself

that tribute that labor must pay to the capitalist." (4) The means of production, even though in this case they are not separated from the worker, already constitute a component part of the circulation of all social capital and in this sense can also be regarded as capital. (5) To a still greater degree, this applies to the case in which the small-scale producer uses hired labor, i.e., directly realizes surplus value on his capital or part of it. This second aspect of small-scale production, namely, the fact that the means of production used in it can on a broad plane be regarded as capital, brings closer together: (1) various types of small-scale production itself and (2) small-scale and factory production, and permits the comparison of economic characteristics of one and the other.

Small-scale production plays a large part in the economy of developing countries, particularly in Asian countries. Between one-third and one-half of the industrial output of these countries is accounted for by small-scale commodity production. Linked to small-scale commodity production is a large group of the independent population which, together with other strata in the urban petty bourgeoisie, constitutes one of the active detachments in the national liberation movements in these countries.

Just as has happened in the countries of "classical" capitalism, the capitalist structure in modern developing countries attempts to crush the resistance and in one case to destroy and in another to subordinate the small-scale commodity structure, to convert it into an additional sphere of capitalist exploitation. However, the economic conditions in former colonies and dependent countries differ from those conditions under which capitalism originated in the Western countries and determine the particular vitality and stability of small-scale commodity production in these countries.

The basic differences are the following.

First, the developing countries set out on the path of independent development after having been exhausted by extended colonial and imperialist exploitation. Primitive accumulation could not and cannot be realized in those forms and at the rate that it was realized in the presently developed capitalist countries. Accordingly, the possibilities of the capitalist structure in these countries are also more limited. In the majority of these countries, the capitalist structure is still unable entirely to control the internal market and is forced to share it with the small-scale commodity structure.

Second, it is impossible to ignore the existence of an enormous mass of "surplus" population in the developing countries, a surplus that cannot be fully employed under existing conditions.

Third, the extremely low cost of manpower and the low effectiveness — from the point of view of the private entrepreneur — of using machines and modern technology deprive the capitalist sector of one of its most powerful stimuli toward expansion. This, in turn, reinforces the vitality of the small-scale commodity structure.

Fourth, as a result of the extended colonial and imperialist exploitation, the economy in most developing countries has become extremely one-sided; there are no stable interbranch relationships that would guarantee the independent and rapid development of the economy; the world market is still a necessary binding link among various branches of the national economy even within one and the same country. At the same time, it is becoming increasingly difficult for developing countries to turn to the world market owing to worsening trade conditions. This circumstance creates additional conditions favorable to the "coexistence" of the capitalist sector with those economic forms that would be crushed by competition under other conditions.

There have also been changes in the social and political conditions under which present-day types of production form and develop in these countries. A more and more active role is played in them by the broad masses, including the urban petty bourgeoisie. The patent inability of the important local bourgeoisie to resolve pressing economic problems and the growth of forces favoring the noncapitalist road of development compel the ruling circles of the developing countries to search for various "middle of the road" ways of economic development, e.g., the development of a government sector of the

economy side by side with the private sector and maneuvering between the interests of large-scale national capital and the interests of the democratic strata in the town and countryside.

Under the changed conditions of economic development in former colonies and dependent countries, things stand differently with respect to the immediate historical fate of small-scale industrial commodity production, its actual and potential role in the economy, and the interrelations between small-scale and factory production.

As we know, the viability of small-scale industrial production is explained to a large extent by the fact that its workers, being content with extremely modest material remuneration, strain their energies to the extreme, stretch their working time to the maximum, require members of the family to participate in the production process, etc. The living standard of the handicraft worker is frequently much lower than that of the factory worker. In the competitive struggle with the factory, he is forced to give up not only the surplus product but also part of the necessary product created at his "enterprise." In many cases, the exploitation of the hired worker in small-scale industry is more brutal and gross than in enterprises of the factory type. In the market as well, the small-scale producer is in a much less advantageous position than the large entrepreneur producing the same product; as a rule, the commodities turned out by small-scale commodity producers are less able to compete and the small-scale producers must bear certain losses in the price on their output. All this does not mean, however, that the sole reason for the survival and preservation of small-scale industry is the ability of small producers to use all manner of means to squirm out of their predicament so as to save their production facility.

Today the question as to the causes underlying the preservation of small-scale production in economically underdeveloped countries is not only of scientific interest. Foreign economists, particularly in the developing countries themselves, during the entire postwar period have persistently raised the question concerning the utilization of small-scale industry as a form of production that promises considerable employment with relatively small outlays of productive capital. There are also opposing views that see the utilization of this form of production as squandering meager national resources. The matter, however, is not limited solely to scientific polemics. In the majority of the developing countries of Asia and in a number of African countries, the support of small-scale and handicraft industries has become the adopted course in government economic policy. It is all the more important to study and compare the basic indicators of the functioning of small-scale and factory industry and to investigate the effectiveness of the one and the other for the national economy of these nations.

It should be emphasized that the present book does not propose to juxtapose small-scale production against factory production. The dominant role of modern highly mechanized enterprises in the industrialization process is indisputable. The author attempts to elucidate the present place of forms of production with a low level of mechanization in the economy of developing countries, their positive and negative sides, and the possibilities for their use in the given stage of construction of the national economy.

* * *

The problem of the employment and use of labor-intensive forms of production is of greatest importance for the developing countries in Asia. In many of them there is colossal open and disguised unemployment and, as a rule, the population growth rate is very high. In a number of African countries as well, considerable attention is given to the development of small-scale industry, which will make for higher employment. Thus in Somalia's five-year plan (1963-1967), one of the basic "social and economic targets" is described as "the development of factory and small-scale industry and crafts." (6) In Kenya's six-year plan (1964-1970), among the top priority projects supported by the government are projects with a high "labor-capital" ratio. (7) As noted in the report of the ECA-FAO

Mission of the United Nations, an important economic problem of Zambia is that of increasing employment of the able-bodied population. (8) The problem of small-scale and handicraft industries is also an urgent one for a number of countries in West Africa. (9)

In certain countries of Africa and Latin America, the problem of using labor-intensive production processes is not as serious as in Asia owing to the much smaller population density and even the "underpopulation" of certain regions. Nonetheless, in these countries as well the problem of using labor-intensive forms is not completely absent because they can prove useful for indicators other than employment and because the shortage of capital is also keenly felt in these countries.

In this book, the analysis of production indicators and various aspects of the economic effectiveness of factory and small-scale industry is made chiefly on the basis of statistical materials of India, Burma, and Pakistan because these materials are the most complete and comprehensive. Unfortunately, statistics on other countries do not permit us to arrive at any kind of coherent idea as to the basic indicators of the activity of small-scale industry and are therefore used only as supplementary illustrative material for the basic conclusions. The author hopes that subsequent research on this important and urgent problem will extend our understanding of it and will introduce into scientific circulation a broader range of statistical materials, including those on other developing countries.

Footnotes

1) We shall conditionally combine small-scale and handicraft industry under the term "small-scale."

2) Of course, it is impossible to encompass the entire diversity of these features. Here only those are cited that have particularly great importance specifically for the present investigation.

3) See V. I. Lenin, Poln. sobr. soch., Vol. 5, p. 136.

8

4) K. Marx and F. Engels, Soch., Vol. 26, part 1, pp. 417-418.

5) See Gorodskie srednie sloi sovremennogo kapitalisticheskogo obshchestva, Moscow, 1963.

6) UN, ECA. Economic and Social Council, Outlines and Selected Indicators of African Development Plans, E/CN, 14/336, January 14, 1965, p. 78. [All quotations from non-Russian sources have been translated from the Russian—Ed.]

7) Ibid., p. 79.

8) Ibid., p. 95.

9) UN, ECA. Economic and Social Council, Report on Activities in Industry, E/CN, 14/298, November 12, 1964, pp. 1-2.

* * *

CHAPTER I

The Role and Specific Features of the Organization of Small-Scale Production in the Developing Countries

The Place of Production with a Low Degree of Mechanization in the Economy

On the basis of purely formal features used for the classification of industry in the majority of developing countries, a certain number of highly mechanized enterprises may fall into small-scale industry. On the whole, however, the statistical data we have used specifically encompass small-scale industry with a low degree of mechanization. In terms of the degree of capital-intensiveness, small-scale and factory industries emerge as two different types of production.

Here are several official definitions of small-scale and cottage industry used in the developing countries. For example, in India small-scale industry includes enterprises with up to 50 workers (if a mechanical engine is used) or up to 100 (if no type of mechanical energy is used) and with a fixed capital less than 500,000 rupees. Of late it has been proposed to delimit this definition of small-scale industry solely by the sum of fixed capital, on the grounds that "one of the principal tasks of small-scale cottage industry is to expand employment and therefore no restriction should be placed on the number of persons employed at a small-scale craft enterprise." (1) In practice, however, the first definition is more frequently used.

According to the definition adopted in Paki-

stan, small-scale industry includes enterprises using or not using hired labor, with up to 50 workers, if no mechanical engine is used, and up to 20 workers if a mechanical engine is used. Enterprises in which members of the family work exclusively or principally are classified under "domestic" [domashnaia] industry as a part of small-scale industry. (2)

In Burma, small-scale industry includes enterprises using not more than 9 hired workers. According to the data of Burma's industrial census, on the average for each small enterprise there are approximately 9 unpaid workers (members of the family). (3)

During the period between 1948-1949 and 1958-1959, the share of small-scale industry in India's national income declined from 10.7 to 8.1%. In absolute figures this income increased from 8.7 billion rupees to 10.1 billion rupees, although this increase was not as great as in the factory industry. As of 1958-1959, small-scale industry accounted for over half of the total national income created in India's industry. The number of persons employed (approximately 12 million) was four times greater than the number of workers in the factory industry. (4) Counting workers who are not fully employed, the number employed in India's small-scale industry reaches 20 million persons. (5)

The most important branches in India's small-scale industry are food, textile, woodworking,

9

glass and ceramics, metalworking, and leather. Not only do these branches concentrate the largest number of workers (see Table 1), but they also create the bulk of the gross national product. Their significance for the economy of the nation is still great. Thus in 1958, India's small-scale industry produced 1,640 million meters or more than one-fourth of all textiles. (6) (See Table 1.) (7)

scale industry accounted for 79% of the national income created in industry. (8) At the present time, small-scale industry has lost its "leading place," but its part is still considerable. During 1961-1962, its share in the national income created in industry constituted approximately 40%. (9) At the present time over 2 million persons are employed in Pakistan's small-scale urban industry and, together with family mem-

Table 1

India. Manpower Distribution by Branch in Small-Scale and Cottage Industry, 1955
(thousands of persons)

Branch	Type of enterprise*			Total
	A	B	C	
Food	2,386	311	75	2,772
Tobacco	240	160	66	466
Cotton	2,725	316	41	3,032
Other branches in the textile industry	1,071	291	82	1,444
Woodworking	1,516	119	21	1,656
Leather and leather goods	535	56	27	618
Glass and ceramics	813	160	59	1,032
Metalworking (excluding machine-building)	732	83	28	843
Jute	57	4	7	68
Printing	25	46	23	94
Chemical	60	60	34	154
Machine-building	106	41	22	169
Other	623	73	10	706
Total	10,889	1,720	495	13,104

*A—enterprises with up to 10 workers (if a mechanical engine is used) or up to 20 (if no mechanical engine is used), principally using the labor of members of the family. B—enterprises with up to 10 or 20 workers, principally based on hired labor. C—enterprises with from 10 to 49 workers (if a mechanical engine is used) or from 20 to 99 (if no engine is used).

During the first years of Pakistan's independent existence, small-scale and cottage production accounted for the bulk of industrial output. Suffice it to say that during 1949-1950, small-bers, come to about 10 million persons. Moreover, a considerable number of those employed

in agriculture are partially employed in cottage industry. According to official data, "domestic" industry "provides partial employment for approximately 90% of the population living in the villages and engaged in unskilled or semiskilled labor." (10)

In Pakistan, weaving is the largest branch of small-scale production. This is followed by the food industry, which is chiefly concentrated in the villages. In recent years, certain economic importance has been acquired by such branches as light chemistry, metalworking, certain types of machine-tool building and the production of spare parts for textile machines. The production of metal utensils, part of which is exported, is an important traditional branch in the small-scale industry of Pakistan. Sporting goods are produced by hand, and more and more importance is attached to the small-scale production of agricultural implements. The latter enjoys special government support. (11)

In 1953, Burma had 31,146 small-scale and cottage enterprises, with a total employment of 92,300 persons. The value of the gross product of these enterprises constituted 143.4 million kyat, or 27.7% of the total gross industrial product; the value added [vnov' sozdannaia stoimost'] was 79.7 million kyat, or approximately 35% of all value added in industry. In all, 98% of the enterprises belonged to persons directly engaged in the production process. The principal branches in Burma's small-scale industry are food, footwear, textile, tobacco, chemical, metal goods, and woodworking. These branches account for 80% of all enterprises, 79% of persons employed, and 78% of all value added in small-scale industry. (12)

In Iran, in 1958, of 107,100 persons employed in industry, 41,100 persons were employed at enterprises with up to 50 persons. (13) The overall number of persons employed in Iran's small-scale industry is unquestionably higher, because manufacture enterprises with more than 50 persons are widespread here. However, manual labor is chiefly used. These enterprises should also be categorized under the heading of small-scale industry.

In Indonesia, in 1939, workers engaged in small-scale and cottage production constituted the majority of all industrial workers — 2.5 million workers out of 3.4 million (including workers in the mining industry). (14) There are no

later summary data. According to a sampling investigation carried out by an ILO Mission in 1958 in urban areas of Java and Madura, handicraft workers and "unpaid" workers — members of their families — constituted 34.4% of the self-employed population of these areas. (15) This does not take account of hired workers employed in small-scale production.

According to the 1937 census, there were approximately 400,000 persons employed in Egypt's small-scale industry, or more than two-thirds of all those employed in industry and construction. Of this number, 176,000 persons were small and independent handicraft workers; over 200,000 workers and employees were employed at small enterprises of the manufacture type, employing between 1 and 9 workers. (16)

The actual number of those employed in Egypt's small-scale industry is greater than the above figure, which does not include workers of enterprises using more than 9 persons. The data of 1955 show that Egypt's industry, which qualifies as large-scale [tsenzovaia] includes a large if not predominant number of small and extremely small enterprises. (17)

It can be seen that certain branches in Egypt's manufacturing industry — in particular, cotton ginning and pressing, food, footwear, and other branches — are distinguished by a very low average employment rate. Knowing the general state of Egyptian industry (obsolescent equipment, extensive use of manual labor, low labor productivity), we may confidently conclude that a number of so-called large-scale enterprises should be categorized under the small-scale industry heading. Unfortunately, it is not possible to isolate these enterprises.

Various types of agricultural crafts are widespread in Egypt. An Egyptian economist, Eva Garzouzi, writes: "There are numerous enterprises and crafts that are popular in Egypt and that can become even more widespread. The most important of these are: the dairy products industry, rug weaving, silkworm breeding, manufacture of baskets and straw mats, drying and preserving fruits and vegetables, manufacture

Table 2

Egypt. Distribution of the Labor Force by Branch in the
"Census Large-Scale" [Tsenzovaia] Industry in 1955

Branch	Number of enterprises	Total number employed (thousands)	Average number of workers per enterprise
Cotton ginning and pressing	93	4.2	45
Food	934	30.9	33
Tobacco	29	6.4	221
Textile	444	89.6	202
Footwear	172	5.1	30
Paper and printing	163	9.2	56
Chemical and petroleum	91	13.6	149
Ferrous metallurgy	71	3.1	44
Machine-building	61	2.4	39
Cement, glass, ceramic	114	8.8	77
Transport equipment	98	9.8	100
Other	422	21.8	52

of clothing for village residents, manufacture of headdress, knitting and embroidery, manufacture of metal utensils, wooden goods, cheap ceramics, etc." (18)

Basic Features in the Organization of Small-Scale Production

The forms of small-scale commodity production, united under the heading "small-scale and cottage industry," are numerous and diverse. Among them are the very ancient and those that have originated in the relatively recent past, small-scale production for a given clientele, and large manufactures working for a broad market.

In economic literature, the most commonly accepted systematization of the forms of production, in terms of the degree of their economic development, is from the lowest to the highest. For the purposes of the present work, however, it is more convenient to classify small-scale production in terms of its role in the process of reproduction of social capital in the countries under investigation. It is precisely from this point of view that the very conditional division

proposed below must be viewed:

(a) "Traditional crafts." This includes, on the one hand, the manual production of custom-made items and luxury items (jewelry, production of custom-made metal and clay utensils, artistic embroidery, wood carving, bone carving, etc.) and, on the other hand, the production of such industrial commodities as can also be manufactured by the factory method. Handmade items, however, are worth more precisely because they are individually manufactured (rugs, furniture, footwear, knitted woolens, certain types of textiles, etc.).

(b) Cottage production of consumer goods. This embraces enterprises based principally on manual labor and manufacturing consumer goods (textiles, foodstuffs, footwear, clothing, toys) that are also produced by factory industry. Some of these enterprises use semifinished goods of factory production and are thus subordinate to the latter and supplement it, while others use their own raw materials and compete with factory industries.

(c) Modern small-scale enterprises, which to a greater or lesser extent use new, even though not the latest, technology and produce modern goods in both the consumer and producer categories. Unlike enterprises in group "b," which are chiefly based on manual labor and which produce consumer goods different from the factory-produced ones, enterprises in this group are better mechanized, sometimes employ an engine, and produce goods that correspond or at least should correspond to factory standards. At the same time, compared with large-scale factory industry, these enterprises are mechanized to a low degree, manual labor is still widely used in them, and, as a rule, the equipment they use is obsolescent.

The boundary separating the latter group of small-scale enterprises from the factory industry is very conditional. Nonetheless, on the whole, owing to its specific features, this group of enterprises should be defined as one of the groups in small-scale industry. The overwhelming majority of enterprises in this group are manufactures even though they have some degree of mechanization.

This classification of the basic forms of small-scale production makes it possible to limit the investigation to those forms that have or can have true national economic significance in the investigated countries and in the reproduction of their social capital.

Enterprises in group "a" — "traditional crafts" — are connected with the overall industrial complex of these countries along two lines. First, they partly use the semifinished products of factory production (rolled nonferrous metals, metal thread, castings, woolen and cotton yarn) for their production. Second, the output of these branches is sold in foreign markets for currency that can be used to purchase equipment and industrial materials.

At the present time, both individual craftsmen and enterprises based on hired labor are engaged in the production of custom-made craft items. The internal demand for these items is to a considerable extent undermined by competition from the cheaper factory and also from imported goods. One sees a trend, however, toward increasing demand for these goods from abroad, and this serves not only to preserve but also to expand this type of production.

The ruling circles of India, Pakistan, and other developing countries are striving to convert the "traditional crafts" into an export branch. In a number of cases this policy has been crowned with success. By way of an example we may cite the manual production of sporting goods, which have become an appreciable item in Pakistan's export. The manual production of sporting goods is concentrated in the city of Sialkot. The government encourages craftsmen from other areas of Pakistan to come to Sialkot. During 1959-1960, the export of handmade sporting goods amounted to more than 11.5 million rupees. (19) In the largest Pakistan cities of Karachi, Lahore, and Dacca the handicraft production of the famous Benares silks is concentrated. In Pakistan, this branch principally was developed after the division, when a large number of refugee craftsmen arrived in the country from India. The weavers are organized in cartels and use primitive manual looms at each of which two persons work — the skilled weaver and his apprentice. The overall number of looms in this branch is 1,500 to 2,000. (20)

It should be noted that the expansion and curtailment of this type of production depend chiefly on such external factors as conditions of the foreign market, the economic policy of the government, etc. It is these things and not the general requirements of reproduction in the country that also determine the possible capital investments in the development of enterprises in group "a." The question as to the economic role of this production and its possibilities compared with factory production is practically not on the agenda. Accordingly, this form can be excluded from the circle of objects in the present investigation.

Enterprises of group "b" — handicraft, chiefly manual, production of consumer goods — are widely represented both in urban and in rural areas in the majority of developing countries. Of these enterprises, those in the food industry concentrate the largest number of workers in small-scale industry in India, Pakistan, and a considerable number of workers in Burma. Most of the food industry enterprises are concentrated in rural areas, and the equipment used is extremely backward and primitive. The greater part of their output (manually husked rice, gur, etc.) is intended for the local market. In most instances, the production is done at home by members of the family. (21)

As of August 1958, India's textile industry numbered 2.6 million handlooms and about 10 million persons, including basic workers and members of their families participating in production. Approximately 72% of all looms in the textile industry are accounted for by the cotton industry. The majority of handloom weavers work on primitive looms with drop [padaiushchii] shuttles. According to the data of a government committee that investigated the situation in handloom weaving, out of all the looms in use, 64% were looms with drop shuttles, 35% had the more efficient flying [letaiushchii] shuttle, and 1% were looms in other categories. (22)

In Pakistan there were 484,500 handlooms during the 1959-1960 period. Of this number, 80% were in the cotton industry and 20% in the silk weaving industry. The overall number employed comprised more than 400,000 persons and, together with working family members, approximately 2 million persons. Handloom weaving provides a considerable part of the total production of cotton textiles in Pakistan. Thus, during 1959-1960, this production was approximately 335 million meters of textiles, while the factory production was 564 million meters. (23) During the period of Pakistan's independence, handloom weaving has increased almost fivefold — from 100,000 to 484,500 looms. As Pakistan economist S. M. Akhtar notes, this growth was chiefly the result of market conditions. (24) The most important of these conditions was the necessity to satisfy at least partially the internal demand for textiles on the basis of internal production. Under those conditions, handmade textiles were not particularly threatened by competition from large-scale production, the more so that the threat of competition from imported textiles was somewhat lessened by protective tariffs. At the present time, however, manually produced textiles are encountering fierce competition from the less expensive factory-produced textiles. In the interests of protecting handloom weaving from competition by factory production, the government has adopted a number of artificial measures, one of which is the prohibition of the production of certain sorts of textiles at factories. These textiles may only be produced at small enterprises. (25)

Small enterprises in group "b" are of great interest from the point of view of their economic effectiveness as a form of production that differs from modern forms of industry, even though on the whole their output is identical to factory output.

Small factories — belonging to group "c" according to the Dhar and Lydall classification — while less widespread, have acquired very great importance in recent years. For India, while employment at enterprises of the groups examined above is in excess of 11 million persons, group "c" accounts for 1.2 million persons. (26)

The small factories spring up side by side with modern factory industry and in a certain sense follow in its footsteps. The great growth of these factories in the investigated countries during the prewar and postwar years (particularly during the period of independence) is explained, first, by the shortage of large-scale capital and, second, by the growing demand of the internal market for both consumer and producer commodities, which the factory industry cannot satisfy. Most frequently the small factory is created on the basis of worn-out and obsolescent equipment whose service life has been used up in the "large-scale" industry; these small factories make extensive use of manual labor. The most important areas of operation of these enterprises in India are the production of beverages, jute goods, paper goods, chemicals and perfumery, small machine equipment, instruments, electrical apparatus, and various spare parts. In Pakistan, the greatest degree of development has been experienced by small enterprises engaged in the production of agricultural implements, hardware items, spare parts for industrial equipment, chemical commodities, etc. As stated above, the market's principal requirement on the output of enterprises in this group is that it be standard and that it equal the quality of goods produced by factory industry. These enterprises are chiefly situated in cities, closer to large-scale industry.

In the present investigation, we are interested in enterprises in groups "b" and "c" and in their economic potential as alternatives to capital-intensive factory production. We shall examine certain problems in their organization.

In India's small-scale industry, the work is done predominantly in the home. Approximately 83% of all workers in small-scale industry are employed in the "domestic" industry. Approximately 13% of the employed are concentrated in small manufactures (up to 20 workers). Enterprises employing up to 5 persons (chiefly members of the family) predominate. This is shown by the following data for 1956. (27)

Type of enterprise with respect to number employed	Number of enterprises (thousands)	Overall number of employed (thousands)
Up to 5	5,000	10,200
5-9	130	910
10-19	43	600
20-49	18	560
50-99	4.7	340

Data of a more particular order — from an investigation of small-scale industry in Moradabad in 1954-1955 — also confirm the fact that the very small enterprises are predominant. Out of the total number of small enterprises in Moradabad, 77.3% were enterprises with 2-4 workers, 16.6% — enterprises with 5-9 workers. From the data in the Moradabad study, it is possible to extract certain additional indicators characterizing small-scale industry. The predominant type is that of the "personal" enterprise in which the owner himself works and uses the labor of members of his family and only in some cases brings in hired manpower. On the whole, for all branches of small-scale industry in Moradabad, this type accounts for 90.3% of the enterprises; partnerships account for 9.5%, and cooperatives represent only 0.13% of the enterprises. (28) In all, 63.3% of the enterprises use

rented land and production buildings, and only 33.1% of the craftsmen work on their own land and in their own home. The bulk of the enterprises (98.9%) are permanent, while seasonal enterprises are characteristic for handicraft production in rural areas.

A specific trait of small-scale industry in Moradabad is that each enterprise performs some single operation toward the production of the finished product. Very seldom is the finished product produced entirely at one enterprise. (29) Another specific feature of Moradabad craftwork is the predominance of manual labor. Of all small-scale enterprises, 91.4% employ manual labor exclusively, and only a few of them to a greater or lesser extent use diesel engines, electric motors, or animal power. "Age-old manufacturing processes based on manual labor have not only survived but offer a marked resistance to modern technology," writes B. Singh, the director of the study in Moradabad. "Sweated labor and extremely low wages coupled with low capital-intensiveness and traditional methods and processes are a marked characteristic of the small-scale industrial sector." (30)

In Pakistan, according to data of a sampling investigation carried out by an ILO mission in 1955, two types of small-scale craft production predominated: domestic craft production and enterprises employing hired labor. (31) For the most part, enterprises of the first type were small (1-6 workers). Enterprises of the second type generally employed 10-19 persons. Essentially, these are already enterprises of the manufacture type. They account for over 70% of all workers employed at the enterprises studied. The greatest percentage of enterprises employing mainly hired labor was in Eastern Pakistan (over 79% of all workers). (32) Thus, in keeping with our classification, most of the investigated enterprises belong to group "b." These are home crafts and manufactures engaged in the production of consumer goods and principally using manual labor. Only 7.6% of the enterprises used an electric motor, and 6.3% of the enterprises made use of other kinds of mechanical energy.

Such a high percentage of manufactures in the overall number of craft enterprises in Pakistan is to no small extent explained by the historical situation accompanying the country's formation. As a result of the division of India and the emigration of Hindu craftsmen from regions going to Pakistan, the primitive Pakistani crafts were destroyed to a considerable extent. In place of the emigrating craftsmen there appeared craftsmen who were refugees from regions of what is today the Indian Union. The majority of them were homeless and without work tools. Not being able to start an independent business, they fell into the net of moneylenders and merchants who supplied them with tools and organized their joint production facility. Out of 4,346 handicraft-manufacture enterprises investigated, 3,240 came into being after 1947. (33) It is precisely this historical situation that also explains, in particular, the high concentration of production in one of the largest branches of Pakistan's small-scale industry — the textile industry. In India, where handlooming is one of the oldest forms of production and where it has not been subjected to such sharp perturbations, production in the home predominates in this branch. In Pakistan, the majority of the manual weavers are employed in enterprises of the manufacture type. "Independent" craftsmen working in families account for approximately one-fifth of the handlooms, and four-fifths of all handlooms are concentrated in organized manufactures; some of them exploit over 100 hired workers. (34)

The bulk of small enterprises in Burma are engaged in production in the home. According to the 1953 census, 98% of all enterprises belonged to persons directly engaged in the production process, and the workers in them were members of their families. At the same time, in the small-scale craft industry of Burma a considerable number of workers are hired workers. For 50,400 "unpaid" workers (members of families) there were 41,800 hired workers. (35) In all other respects, the organization of small-scale production in Burma is close to the Indian.

Exploitation of Small-Scale Production by Moneylenders and Merchants

One of the most important features in small-scale industry is the existence of a far-flung network of parasitic middlemen. While the organized manufacture unites craftsmen who have completely fallen into the hands of moneylenders or merchants, the majority of "independent" small producers working at home are in fact only nominally independent, even though the forms and the degree of their dependence on the middlemen may be different. In terms of the degree of dependence of craftsmen on middlemen, we can isolate three types of small-scale production organization: (1) the formally independent craftsman working in his own home and independently managing production and sales. He receives occasional loans from the moneylender, however, and is linked to him only with respect to repaying the loan and the interest on it; (2) the craftsman engaging in production on a broader scale involving the use of hired manpower; the raw materials and sometimes the means of production are made available by the middleman (moneylender-merchant); (3) a small industrial enterprise managed either by a former craftsman or by a merchant who "has changed from a middleman for selling the output into the owner of the enterprise itself"; workers at these enterprises are hired. (36)

According to the materials of an official investigation of the handloom weaving industry, conducted in India in 1941, "independent" craftsmen numbered 978,700 persons; weavers working on the basis of orders and using raw materials provided by the moneylenders numbered 535,400; workers in "karkhana" — 158,300; members of cooperative societies — 26,300 persons. (37) In the period that has elapsed since 1941, there has been a differentiation in the composition of handicraft weavers both with respect to their increased dependence on middlemen as well as with respect to a certain increase in their membership in cooperative societies. By 1959, the cooperatives possessed 193,000 handlooms out of the total 515,000 looms in small-scale industry. (38) While the cooperative societies supported by the government are to a greater or lesser extent protected against the middleman, the "unorganized" craftsmen are utterly defenseless before him. The same source reports: "One of the 'evils' of the system of middlemen in the handloom weaving industry is that the middleman 'buys cheap and sells dear.' This is possible only because the handloom weaver, provided he is not a member of a cooperative society, is in the clutches of the merchant, moneylender, or master from the ranks of the craftsmen, depending on the circumstances." (39)

Facts from the investigation of small-scale industry in Moradabad (India) give a clear idea of the scope of the middleman's activities. Some of the polled middlemen here simultaneously cover 1,000-2,000 craftsmen. In turn, many large middlemen operate through agents, so-called dalals. On the average, each such middleman employs 29-30 dalals. (40)

As a result of the process of property differentiation of many years' standing and also the "aid" of moneylenders and merchants, a considerable part of the craftsmen have lost their basic means of production and already from the very beginning of the production process are firmly chained to the middleman. According to the data of an investigation carried out by Madras University, in the state of Madras "all weavers employed in manufactures and 'karkhana' and 27.8% of the weavers working at home do not have looms." (41) Even for subsistence, the craftsmen are forced to turn to the moneylender for "aid." According to the same data cited above, "in order to obtain the means of subsistence, the weaver is forced to resort to loans in the average sum of 32 rupees (which constitutes 40% of the total outlays for subsistence)."(42)

Particularly great is the dependence of craftsmen (even those who have their own implements and means of production) on middlemen for the supplying of raw materials and for selling the finished output. This applies first and foremost to craftsmen living in areas that are remote from industrial centers and to craftsmen depending on imported materials. The middleman

system of supplying the craftsman with the necessary materials is described as follows in the monograph by Indian economist Farooquee: "If the craftsmen use materials that must be obtained from the city, they generally acquire them through a middleman...the latter exploits the ignorance and indebtedness of the craftsman. He not only exacts a higher price for the material; he also employs fraudulent tactics, mixing low-quality and high-quality materials." (43)

For the craftsman, as a rule, the problem of raw materials supply is connected with the necessity of obtaining credit because he does not have free sums that could serve in the capacity of working capital. According to the data of the Moradabad study, over 40% of all investigated enterprises were compelled to obtain raw materials entirely on credit, while about 25% of the enterprises met 50-75% of their need for raw materials on the basis of credit. (44) The study Capital for Medium and Small-Scale Industries openly states: "The very small enterprises suffer from a shortage of working capital and experience difficulty in obtaining long-term credit. But regarding short-term credit, the moneylenders are the only source." (45)

In the overwhelming majority of cases, such deals are concluded under the most disadvantageous conditions and usually stipulate that the output be sold specifically to the lender — the moneylender or merchant. As repeatedly stated in the works of numerous investigators, the interest rates for credit from moneylenders are utterly exorbitant. But even if the moneylender charges relatively small interest on the loans, he more than rewards himself through the business deal with the craftsman. Frequently, excessively high prices for raw materials and underpayments to the craftsman for his output mask an excessively high interest rate on the loan. (46)

Thus, in the words of P. N. Dhar, "the wholesale merchant...embodies the entire external economic world for the small commodity producer. One of the apparent results of this dependence is that the conditions of trade are always against the small producer." (47)

The same holds true for Pakistan. "Small enterprises cannot obtain raw materials under acceptable conditions," the first five-year plan of Pakistan states. "They buy small quantities of raw materials through middlemen for prices that are much higher than those paid by large enterprises. It happens that the small producers are also dependent on the middleman for credit, and this forces them to go deeply into debt and to be tied to the same middlemen no matter what prices they name. Further, under present conditions, when a shortage of foreign currency is felt and the system of import license favors merchants more than producers, it is very difficult for small enterprises to obtain imported materials. Even if these materials can be obtained, the shortage of them finds its expression in the prices and profits of the middlemen.... Being dependent upon the middleman with respect to credit, the small producer is compelled to sell him his output for any price the latter offers." The plan points out that as a result of the dependence on the middleman for raw material, sales, and credit, the small commodity producer is barely able to provide himself with the means of subsistence. (48)

In other investigations, the dependence of the Pakistani craftsman on the middleman is described in still stronger language. Thus, sometimes the weavers are compelled to pay 25-50% more for factory-produced yarn than weaving mills pay. The authors of the study entitled The Economy of Pakistan write: "The situation is still worse for the craftsman if the raw material must be shipped over great distances or if the cost of the raw material is very high.... In those cases, the craftsman is entirely in the power of the merchant who exploits him both in shipping the raw materials and in purchasing his output. The merchant literally holds him in slavery because at the same time he is the creditor who extends loans for the everyday needs of the craftsman and his family." (49)

It is impossible to cite an accurate figure describing the number of middlemen working in small-scale industry in India and Pakistan. Nonetheless, even from the foregoing it becomes clear that there must be a very considerable number of them, and that small-scale production is literally being crushed under the burden of merchant-moneylender's capital. In this connection it is important to emphasize that the enormous army of parasitic middlemen receives more than a "good" rate of interest on their capital, notwithstanding the backward and inefficient methods of small-scale production and the extremely low labor productivity of small-scale commodity producers.

One of the important aspects concerning the present position of small-scale production is its relationship to the factory industry. Many branches of small-scale industry in groups "b" and "c," by the very nature of their output and the raw materials used by them, are forced to compete with the factory. It is known that this competition undermines the very roots of small-scale industry's existence — the conditions under which one and the other side find themselves are too unequal. It is sufficient to mention the sharp differences in labor productivity between small-scale and the factory industry. "... the technical backwardness of this (small-scale — S. K.) industry raises the costs of production and makes it impossible for it to compete with large-scale industry." (50)

In competing with factory industry, small-scale production loses a considerable amount on the difference between the cost and market price of the commodity. It also incurs considerable losses in the process of purchasing raw materials. Large entrepreneurs intercept scarce imported raw materials, in particular, thus forcing the small entrepreneurs to be content with low quality materials "for utterly unreasonable prices." (51) As the facts show, in Pakistan even the cooperative societies are more poorly supplied with raw materials than the factory enterprises. (52)

Side by side with the sharp competition between small-scale and factory industry, one observes a pronounced trend toward symbiosis between them under the factory's command. This is expressed first of all in the fact that the craftsmen have begun to make use of semifinished goods manufactured by large-scale industry. This is particularly apparent in handlooming in which factory-produced yarn is used. It is known that Indian manual weavers, despite government attempts to revive handspinning, prefer to use factory-made yarn. In view of the acute demand for factory yarn both from the small commodity producers and from the weaving mills, in a number of states the Indian government has been forced to assume control over its distribution. (53)

As regards Pakistan, as a rule, the craftsman-weavers use factory-made yarn. Handspinning has lost almost all importance and continues to exist here and there in Punjab and Eastern Bengal, chiefly in the villages. According to the 1951 census, only 5,200 persons were engaged in handspinning. Since that time, the significance of this craft has declined still further. (54) In a number of cases, manufactures working with the semifinished products of factory production can be regarded as appendages of the factories. In these cases, the factories are oriented toward selling their output to craftsmen. Thus, approximately 60% of the woolen yarn (approximately 415,000 kg) produced by a factory in Harnai [?] (Western Pakistan) goes to supply craftsmen of this region for the manual production of rugs, blankets, and other goods. (55)

The link between small-scale and factory production is also expressed in the fact that small-scale enterprises, in turn, manufacture various kinds of semifinished goods or individual components of items for large-scale production. It cannot be said that this integration is of a completely organized or mass nature, but nonetheless it does have a certain economic significance, the more so that the policy — e.g., of the Indian government and also of Pakistan — is oriented toward promoting the creation of ancillary small enterprises for large-scale industry. (56) According to the data of P. N. Dhar, the share of Delhi's small-scale industry output delivered to the factory industry equalled 6.2% in the printing industry, 7.4% in light machine-building, 15.9% in metallurgy, 17.4% in the production of electric commodities, and 19.6% in general machine-building. (57)

The powerful bourgeoisie in India and Pakistan is striving to subordinate small-scale production to its influence, to incorporate it in the sphere of capitalist exploitation. This is seen if only in the fact that in the last decade there has been a definite increase in the percentage of bank credits going to small-scale industry in the overall sum of bank credits to industry. According to the data of the Reserve Bank of India, in 1952 this share constituted only 10.8%, while by September 1957 it had already risen to 30%. (58) Previously, commercial banks had preferred to deal with big urban moneylenders and middlemen in small-scale industry.

It should be noted that the process of subordinating small-scale production to large-scale production, a process that is generally inevitable in capitalist society, proceeds at a relatively slow rate in the investigated countries as a result of a number of opposing factors. The most important factors among these are: the dispersed nature of small-scale production, which makes the factory's control over it ineffectual; its dependence on moneylenders' capital and middlemen (figuratively speaking, frequently it is simply disadvantageous for a large entrepreneur to sustain this entire parasitic army); and finally, the craftsmen themselves powerfully resist being swallowed up by the factory.

Footnotes

1) P. N. Dhar and H. F. Lydall, The Role of Small Enterprises in Indian Economic Development, Bombay, 1961, pp. 8-9.
2) J. Russell Andrus and Azizali F. Mohammed, The Economy of Pakistan, London, 1958, p. 190; Pakistan Trade, July 1959, p. 42.
3) Union of Burma, First Stage Census 1953, Vol. 2: "Industry, Cottage Industry, and Home-Consumed Production Industry," Rangoon, 1958.
4) Perspective, June 1961, No. 2.
5) India. A Reference Annual, 1955. Delhi, 1955, p. 266.
6) Handloom Weaving Industry in India with Special Reference to Madras State, New Delhi, 1960, p. 1; The Indian Cotton Textile Industry (1957-1958 Annual), Vol. XX, Bombay, January 1959, p. 10.

20

7) Dhar and Lydall, op. cit., p. 5.

8) "The Budget 1960/61," Economic Survey and Statistics, April 1959-March 1960," Karachi, 1960, p. 2.

9) Pakistan—Basic Facts, Karachi, 1963, p. 105.

10) Government-Sponsored Corporations, Ministry of Finance (Economic Affairs Division), Government of Pakistan, Karachi, 1959, p. 74.

11) The Pakistan Times, July 22, 1961.

12) Union of Burma, First Stage Census 1953, Vol. 2, pp. 30, 51-60.

13) Industry and Mines Statistical Yearbook 1958-1959, Teheran, 1959.

14) Economic Survey of Asia and the Far East, 1948, New York, 1949, pp. 109-110.

15) ILO Report to the Government of Indonesia on Labor Statistics, Geneva, 1962, p. 91.

16) See L. A. Fridman, Kapitalisticheskoe razvitie Egipta, Moscow, 1963, pp. 164, 168.

17) Eva Garzouzi, Old Ills and New Remedies in Egypt, Cairo, 1957, p. 60.

18) Ibid., p. 63.

19) Pakistan Trade, Vol. XI, No. 10, October 1960, p. 238.

20) Pakistan Quarterly, Vol. VII, No. 3, 1958, pp. 38-43.

21) Dhar and Lydall, op. cit., p. 2.

22) Handloom Weaving Industry in India, New Delhi, 1960, pp. 1-3.

23) Pakistan Trade, Vol. XI, No. 10, October 1960, p. 113.

24) S. M. Akhtar, Economics of Pakistan, Vol. II, Lahore, 1961, p. 32.

25) Pakistan Trade, Vol. XI, No. 10, October 1960, p. 113; S. M. Akhtar, Economics of Pakistan, Vol. II, p. 33.

26) Dhar and Lydall, op. cit., p. 8.

27) Ibid., p. 7.

28) Baljit Singh, The Economics of Small-Scale Industries. A Case Study of Small-Scale Industrial Establishments of Moradabad, Bombay, 1961.

29) Ibid., pp. 12, 13, 14.

30) Ibid., pp. 14-15.

31) Report of the ILO on Manpower Survey in Pakistan (November 21, 1954 to April 17, 1956), Karachi, 1958, p. 81.

32) Ibid.

33) Ibid., p. 80.

34) S. M. Akhtar, Economics of Pakistan, Vol. II, p. 32; The First Five-Year Plan 1955-1960, Karachi, 1958, p. 476.

35) Union of Burma, First Stage Census 1953, Vol. II, p. 30.

36) Dhar, Small-Scale Industries in Delhi, Bombay, 1958, pp. 7-8.

37) Handloom Weaving Industry in India . . ., p. 10.

38) Ibid., p. 50.

39) Ibid., p. 54.

40) Singh, op. cit., p. 97.

41) Handloom Weaving Industry in India . . ., p. 59.

42) Ibid., p. 53.

43) Q. N. Farooquee, Small-Scale and Cottage Industries as a Means of Providing Better Opportunities for Labour in India, Aligarh, 1958, p. 17.

44) Singh, op. cit., p. 100.

45) Capital for Medium and Small-Scale Industries, Bombay, 1959, p. 31.

46) Dhar, op. cit., p. 42.

47) Ibid., p. 49; Handloom Weaving Industry in India . . ., p. 53.

48) The First Five-Year Plan 1955-1960, Karachi, 1958, pp. 471-472.

49) Andrus and Mohammed, op. cit., p. 201.

50) Farooquee, op. cit., p. 17.

51) Andrus and Mohammed, op. cit., p. 201.

52) The Pakistan Times, January 9, 1961.

53) Handloom Weaving Industry in India . . ., p. 58.

54) Andrus and Mohammed, The Economy of Pakistan, op. cit., p. 192.

55) Pakistan Moves Forward. Textile Industry, Karachi, 1955, p. 22.

56) K. T. Ramakrishna, Finances for Small-Scale Industry in India, Bombay, 1962, p. 18.

57) Dhar, op. cit., p. 46.

58) Ramakrishna, op. cit., p. 48.

* * *

CHAPTER II

Comparison of the Structure of Capital and Labor Productivity in Small-Scale Industry and in Factory Industry [1]

Fixed Capital

The amount of fixed capital per worker [tekhnicheskaia vooruzhennost' truda] serves as one of the most important characteristics for technological modes of production that differ in degrees of labor-intensiveness. Most branches in India's manufacturing industry are characterized by a considerable gap between the amounts of the fixed capital used in factory industry as compared with small-scale industry, even though this gap is not uniform in different branches. Thus, in the production of electric goods, the fixed capital of the factory industry is only 2.2 times greater than the fixed capital used in small-scale industry; in the chemical and pharmaceutical branches the gap is 8.2 times; in the flour milling branch — 9.8 times; in the soap-making industry — more than 14 times; and this gap is most pronounced in the metallurgical branch — 48.6 times (see Table 3).

In Pakistan's manufacturing industry, the gap between the amounts of fixed capital in the factory and small-scale industry is not as considerable as in India (see Table 4); except for the footwear branch, in which the gap in the amounts of fixed capital between the two types of industrial production is 5.3 times, and the glass industry, where the gap is tenfold, it is insignificant. In the food industry, the fixed capital per worker in the factory industry is 1.8 times greater than the corresponding index for small-scale production in this branch; in the textile branch — 1.3 times; in the chemical branch — 2.3; in the cement branch — 2.4 times; in the production of metal goods — only 17%; in the production of plastics — 22%; and in machine-building — 13%. The leather industry is an exception: the fixed capital in the leather industry at small enterprises is very great — 13,650 rupees per worker — and exceeds the fixed capital at factory enterprises in this branch by 4.5 times.

The fact that the gap in the amounts of fixed capital per worker in Pakistan is not as great as in India can be explained, in particular, by the fact that the data we are using on small-scale industry in Pakistan refer to industry of the city of Karachi, where the level of mechanization (including that of numerous small enterprises) is considerably higher than for the nation as a whole, particularly if we consider craft enterprises and individual craftsmen scattered throughout the rural areas. Moreover, many small Pakistani enterprises were created in the relatively recent past and therefore are better technically equipped than small old enterprises in India. In certain cases, particularly in such branches as machine-building, on the basis of the characteristics of large-scale industry, small industrial enterprises with a high organic composition of capital fall into the category of small enterprises, while in terms of labor productivity they actually do not differ

Table 3

India. Basic Economic Indices of the Factory Industry (A) and Small-Scale (B) Industry

(rupees per worker)

Branch and type of industry		Fixed capital	Working capital	Total invested capital (K)	Annual wage fund (V*)	Annual value of processed raw material (R)	Annual value of gross product (P)	Annual net product (y)	Annual surplus product (m)	"Gross output-capital" ratio $\left(\frac{P}{K}\right)$	"Net output-capital" ratio $\left(\frac{y}{K}\right)$	Annual surplus-value norm $\left(\frac{m}{V}\right)$	Annual profit norm $\left(\frac{m}{K}\right)$
Flour milling	A	4,600	4,550	9,150	1,310	47,435	53,700	4,300	2,990	5.9	0.47	2.30	0.33
	B	470	1,220	1,690	706	5,600	7,400	1,230	524	4.4	0.73	0.74	0.31
Production of vegetable oils	A	2,720	3,880	6,600	680	25,695	28,700	1,750	1,070	4.3	0.26	1.57	0.16
	B	435	875	1,310	742	12,800	14,700	1,150	408	11.2	0.88	0.55	0.31
Soap making	A	6,000	11,550	17,550	2,520	21,160	40,000	12,750	10,230	2.3	0.73	4.07	0.58
	B	420	2,520	2,940	882	14,200	17,800	2,000	1,618	6.0	0.85	1.85	0.55
Chemical and pharmaceutical	A	8,970	6,550	15,520	1,910	8,157	16,610	6,150	4,240	1.1	0.40	2.20	0.27
	B**	1,090	1,130	2,220	551	960	3,950	1,340	789	1.8	0.60	1.43	0.35
General machine-building	A	2,600	3,300	5,900	1,550	4,998	8,100	3,040	1,490	1.4	0.52	0.96	0.25
	B	970	1,610	2,580	1,130	2,320	4,700	1,730	600	1.8	0.67	0.53	0.23
Electrical commodities	A	2,430	3,860	6,290	1,750	5,297	9,050	3,200	1,450	1.4	0.51	0.83	0.23
	B	1,100	1,500	2,600	1,580	5,350	8,650	2,590	1,010	3.3	1.00	0.64	0.39
Metal casting	A	14,100	5,550	19,650	2,430	7,147	14,200	5,210	2,780	0.7	0.26	1.14	0.14
	B	290	300	590	703	380	1,360	765	62	2.3	1.30	0.09	0.10
Light machine-building	A	3,700	2,590	6,290	2,705	5,166	11,000	5,158	2,453	1.7	0.82	0.83	0.39
	B	610	565	1,175	819	1,920	360	1,210	391	3.1	1.03	0.47	0.33

*In calculating V in small-scale industry, we shall conditionally consider that the members of the craftsman's family receive payment equal to the wages of hired workers.

**Pharmaceutical only.

Sources: P.H. Dhar, Small-Scale Industries in Delhi, pp. 23, 27, 50, 57, 61, 63, 77; Thirteenth Census of Indian Manufactures 1958, Calcutta, 1961, pp. 7-18, 373; Bhabatosh Datta, The Economics of Industrialization, Calcutta, 1960, p. 226; Economic Survey for Asia and the Far East, Bangkok, 1961, p. 24.

from large-scale enterprises of the manufacturing industry.

According to the data of the 1953 industrial census of Burma, in a number of branches of the manufacturing industry (tobacco, footwear, furniture) the amount of fixed capital per employed person is approximately equal both in the factory industry and in small-scale industry. The greatest gap is observed in the woodworking branch, where this gap is more than 10 times greater at factory enterprises than in small enterprises; in the textile industry it is 7.2 and in the metal goods industry — 5.4 times. In 4 out of 17 branches investigated in the manufacturing industry of Burma, the amount of fixed capital per worker is higher in small-scale industry. On the average, the amount of fixed capital throughout all branches of Burma's manufacturing industry is 3.9 times higher in the factory industry as compared with small-scale industry (see Table 5).

As we can see, the difference between fixed capital per worker in the factory and small-scale industry of Burma is less than in India's industry and is approximately at the level of Pakistan's manufacturing industry. Here, however, the reasons will be somewhat different. In Burma, there is a lower level of fixed capital per worker in the factory industry. Accordingly, on the basis of this index, factory industry would seem to be on the same footing with small-scale industry with a low-degree mechanization. Such branches as the tobacco, furniture, paper, rubber, nonmetallic goods, and metallurgical branches are distinguished by a particularly low level of capital per worker.

As the data show, at the present time the functional distribution of capital is more effective in the factory industry. Thus, according to the data of the National Sample Survey conducted by the Indian Statistical Institute, in India's small-scale industry land and buildings constituted 45.2% of the value of fixed capital and 33.5% in the factory industry. (2) According to the data from an investigation of the small-scale and cottage industry in Moradabad, the share of land and buildings in the value of fixed capital was still more considerable. On the average, through-

out all investigated branches, 79.5% of the value of fixed capital was accounted for by land and buildings, approximately 18% by machines and equipment, and the remaining portion represented the share of electric power, etc. In certain branches of the investigated small-scale industry, the share of land and buildings in fixed capital was still greater than the above average figure, e.g., 98.8% in metal engraving; 91.9% in the leather, tobacco, and textile industries; and 96.9% in the production of ceramics. (3) "Approximately four-fifths of all fixed capital (of small enterprises — S. K.) are in the form of land and buildings. In fact, for many of these enterprises this is all the fixed capital they own," (4) notes Baljit Singh, director of the study in Moradabad.

Unquestionably, within small-scale industry as well there are great differences in the functional distribution of capital.

As pointed out above, very frequently the land and buildings that make up a part of fixed capital of a small enterprise are not the property of the owner of this enterprise. Because, in assessing fixed capital, some authors include the total value of buildings and the land, while others only include the rent payment for them, it is not surprising that the structure of fixed capital is also different in various studies. However, even proceeding from the most general conceptions as to the lowest forms of industrial production — their scattered nature and the resulting "uneconomical nature," the predominance or considerable share of manual labor equipped only with the most primitive instruments, etc. — it can be assumed that the data of the statistical institute and Baljit Singh are close to reality. In other words, expenditures of an ancillary nature (for renting land and buildings) are relatively greater in small-scale industry.

Of course, this general principle may prove to be insufficient for solving problems of national planning. For the summary evaluation of the effectiveness of one or another technological mode of production, the need may arise for a more precise determination of the comparative advantage of one or another structure of the fixed capital.

Branch and type of industry		Fixed capital	Working capital	Total invested capital (K)	Annual wage fund (V*)
Food	A	4,512	3,780	8,280	1,241
	B	2,500	690	3,190	1,110
Textile	A	4,144	1,880	6,030	997
	B	3,118	1,720	4,840	889
Of which:					
Cotton	A	4,201	2,200	6,400	1,044
	B	1,887	870	2,650	849
Silk weaving	A	3,908	1,430	5,330	1,065
	B	3,685	1,360	5,040	906
Footwear	A	1,495	1,800	3,300	1,832
	B	441	1,280	1,895	1,160
Leather	A	3,014	4,900	7,920	1,072
	B	13,655	6,640	20,290	1,471
Chemical	A	6,891	2,900	9,700	1,240
	B	2,865	2,100	4,970	1,433
Of which:					
Perfumery, cosmetics, soap making, etc.	A	3,496	3,500	7,060	916
	B	1,878	1,700	3,570	1,167
Glass, ceramics	A	2,784	980	3,780	838
	B	279	1,800	2,080	1,059
Cement	A	4,550	1,850	6,400	936
	B	1,854	1,750	3,600	537
Metal goods	A	2,420	1,920	4,340	1,017
	B	2,035	975	3,015	967
Machine-building (excluding electric machine-building)	A	2,299	1,350	3,650	942
	B	2,612	2,220	4,820	1,335
Plastics production	A	3,133	1,600	4,740	897
	B	2,569	1,000	3,560	1,007

*Amortization in the amount (conditional) of 10% of fixed capital is subtracted.

Source: Census of Manufacturing Industries, 1957; Statistical Bulletin, December 1959, Vol. 7, pp. Vol. 8, February 1960, pp. 314-317.

Table 4

Factory (A) and Small-Scale (B) Industry
per worker)

Annual value of processed raw material (R)	Annual value of gross product (P)	Annual net product (y)	Annual surplus product (m)	"Gross output-capital" ratio $\left(\dfrac{P}{K}\right)$	"Net output-capital" ratio $\left(\dfrac{y}{K}\right)$	Annual surplus value norm $\left(\dfrac{m}{V}\right)$	Annual profit norm $\left(\dfrac{m}{K}\right)$
17,405	21,200	3,750	2,509	2.6	0.45	2.02	0.30
13,074	15,700	2,350	1,260	4.9	0.74	1.15	0.39
3,673	6,000	1,980	985	1.0	0.33	0.99	0.16
3,313	5,150	1,760	870	1.1	0.36	0.98	0.18
3,745	6,350	2,200	1,160	1.1	0.34	1.11	0.34
2,059	3,760	1,730	880	1.4	0.65	1.03	0.65
2,604	5,000	2,200	1,140	0.9	0.41	1.08	0.21
1,926	3,740	1,000	95	0.7	0.18	0.10	0.02
5,541	9,350	3,700	1,870	2.8	1.12	1.02	0.57
2,592	4,200	1,610	450	2.2	0.85	0.39	0.24
6,280	12,000	2,700	1,630	1.5	0.34	1.52	0.21
27,437	36,700	7,935	6,465	1.8	0.39	4.40	0.32
4,407	7,650	2,500	1,270	0.8	0.26	1.03	0.13
11,156	16,200	2,200	770	3.3	0.44	0.54	0.15
9,066	12,200	2,600	1,680	1.7	0.37	1.83	0.24
13,977	17,000	2,850	1,680	4.8	0.80	1.44	0.47
1,576	2,900	1,050	210	0.8	0.28	0.25	0.06
1,956	3,350	1,370	310	1.6	0.66	0.29	0.15
1,747	3,550	1,350	410	0.6	0.21	0.44	0.06
1,561	3,150	1,385	845	0.9	0.39	1.56	0.23
3,868	5,850	1,860	840	1.3	0.43	0.82	0.19
2,621	4,660	1,780	810	1.5	0.59	0.83	0.27
2,719	4,500	1,800	860	1.2	0.49	0.91	0.24
2,915	4,270	1,730	400	0.9	0.36	0.30	0.08
3,008	5,050	1,760	860	1.1	0.37	0.96	0.18
2,046	4,600	2,280	1,280	1.3	0.64	1.28	0.36

1580-1585; Census of Small-Scale Manufacturing Industries, Karachi, 1958; Statistical Bulletin,

Table 5

Burma. Basic Economic Indices of Factory Industry (A) and Small-Scale (B) Industry

(kyats per worker)

Branch and type of industry		Fixed capital	Annual wage fund $(V*)$	Annual value of processed raw materials (R)	Annual value of gross product (P)	Annual net product $(y**)$	Annual surplus product (m)	"Gross output-capital" ratio $\left(\frac{P***}{K}\right)$	"Net output-capital" ratio $\left(\frac{y}{K}\right)$	Annual norm of surplus value $\left(\frac{m}{V}\right)$
Average for the total manufacturing industry	A	1,107	476	2,636	5,562	1,529	1,053	5.02	1.48	2.22
	B	286	420	840	1,704	835	415	5.96	3.02	0.99
Food	A	1,690	494	3,687	5,626	1,770	1,276	3.33	1.15	2.58
	B	563	435	1,341	2,565	1,168	733	4.56	2.17	1.68
Tobacco	A	108	330	857	1,772	904	574	16.40	8.47	1.74
	B	106	289	613	1,409	784	495	13.29	7.50	1.71
Textile	A	1,314	396	2,689	5,157	2,337	1,941	3.92	1.88	4.90
	B	179	369	1,003	1,698	677	308	9.49	3.88	0.83
Footwear	A	265	492	1,663	3,291	1,601	1,109	12.42	6.14	2.25
	B	254	502	776	1,717	916	414	6.76	3.70	0.82
Woodworking (excluding furniture)	A	1,447	574	1,537	2,923	1,241	667	2.02	0.96	1.16
	B	136	298	288	719	417	119	5.29	3.17	0.40
Furniture	A	219	360	546	1,330	761	401	6.07	3.58	1.11
	B	208	561	595	1,665	1,049	488	8.00	5.14	0.87

Paper	A	134	220	335	866	517	297	6.46	3.96	1.35
	B	83	341	223	664	433	92	8.00	5.31	0.27
Printing	A	1,399	1,312	2,108	4,903	2,655	1,343	3.50	2.00	1.02
	B	2,269	829	517	1,824	1,078	249	0.80	0.58	0.30
Leather	A	966	1,027	9,527	12,085	2,461	1,434	12.51	2.65	1.40
	B	621	812	1,907	3,523	1,555	743	5.67	2.60	0.91
Rubber	A	111	337	492	1,137	634	297	10.24	5.81	0.88
	B	929	521	908	1,773	772	251	1.91	0.93	0.48
Chemical	A	1,525	391	5,297	7,030	1,594	1,203	4.61	1.14	3.08
	B	467	357	1,921	2,925	957	600	6.26	2.15	1.68
Petroleum refining, coke-gas industry	A	1,351	919	622	1,703	946	27	1.26	8.01	0.03
	B	739	295	1,964	3,043	1,006	711	4.12	1.46	2.41
Glass, ceramics, etc.	A	77	192	185	618	425	233	8.02	5.62	1.21
	B	90	466	156	910	745	279	10.11	8.38	0.60
Metallurgical	A	407	1,099	1,827	3,173	1,305	206	7.80	3.31	0.19
	B	579	660	500	1,484	926	266	2.56	1.70	0.40
Metal goods production	A	1,691	613	2,156	3,779	1,454	841	2.23	0.96	1.37
	B	312	473	597	1,459	830	357	4.68	2.76	0.75
Machine-building	A	2,768	598	268	1,259	705	107	0.45	0.35	0.18
	B	1,514	573	338	1,081	599	26	0.71	0.50	0.05
Transport equipment	A	626	760	2,014	2,833	756	-4	4.61	1.31	-0.01
	B	326	390	473	1,142	635	245	3.50	2.05	0.63

*In calculating V in small-scale industry, we conditionally consider that members of the craftsman's family receive payment equal to wages of hired workers.

**Amortization in the amount (conditional) of 10% of fixed capital is subtracted.

***Owing to the absence of data on working capital, indices of the capital-output ratio and others are calculated per unit of fixed capital.

Source: Union of Burma, First Stage Census 1953, Vol. 2, pp. 51-60, 84-85.

28

In our opinion, such determination first requires the development of a uniform approach to the assessment of the components of fixed capital. This is not an easy question because several variants are known for assessing fixed capital and its components — in particular, in terms of the cost of acquisition; in current prices (revaluation of assets); considering solely rent payments; considering both the value of all fixed capital as well as rent payments irrespective of whether the elements of fixed capital are owned or rented. Clearly, no matter which variant is chosen, it must be uniform for all compared enterprises. Second, the compared branches and enterprises must have production conditions that are maximally similar (same kind of output, assortment, initial raw material, etc.).

Working Capital

In India, the gap in the amounts of working capital per worker in enterprises of the factory and small-scale industry is less than in the case of fixed capital. The maximum gap — 18 times — is observed in the metallurgical industry. In all other investigated branches the gap is 2-4 times.

In the factory industry of Pakistan, the maximum amount of working capital is 5.5 times greater than in small-scale industry (food branch). For the majority of branches, this gap is no greater than 1.5-2 times, while in certain branches of small-scale industry the amount of working capital per worker is even higher than in the factory industry (for example, in the leather, glass-ceramic, and machine-building industries).

It can be noted that in many branches of industry in India and Pakistan, the amount of working capital per unit of fixed capital is higher in small-scale industry. In other words, to service (the function of working capital can so be viewed), or to put into operation a given mass of the means of labor, requires more working capital in small-scale industry than in factory industry. As a matter of fact, this could be expected, pro-

ceeding from the very conditions of small-scale production — its fractional nature, unfavorable position in the market, etc. At the same time, we can take another approach to the problem of working capital that also makes sense under certain conditions. This approach takes the form of comparing technological modes in terms of the amount of working capital required for the production of a unit of output. We shall dwell on this point in somewhat greater detail.

As we know, other conditions being equal, a greater amount of working capital is evidence either of the unfavorable conditions of the production unit itself, which is forced to keep excess funds in working capital elements, or of the unfavorable position of a given enterprise or production unit in the system of market relations.

In itself, however, the amount of an enterprise's working capital cannot serve as an indicator of the effectiveness of its work. It is a dependent value, a complex function of the fixed capital. As Marx noted, "The value of working capital — in the form of the labor force and means of production — is advanced only for the time during which the product is manufactured; moreover, it is advanced in accordance with the scale of production, determined by the size of the fixed capital." (5) Accordingly, the ratio of working capital to the volume of production or to the value of gross product is an important index that characterizes production from the point of view of working capital used. The smaller this ratio, the more advantageous is the production.

In the manufacturing industry of India, the "working capital-output" ratio is more favorable for small-scale industry, i.e., the amount of working capital at small enterprises is relatively less than at enterprises in the factory industry. Only the flour milling industry constitutes an exception (see Table 6).

In the manufacturing industry of Pakistan, the picture is more varied. In the food, leather, and chemical industries and in the production of metal goods and plastics, the "working capital-output" ratio is less at small enterprises. In other branches, on the other hand, this ratio is higher

Table 6

India. Pakistan. "Working Capital-Output" Ratio in Various Branches
of the Factory (A) and Small-Scale (B) Industry

India			Pakistan		
Branch and type of industry		"Working capital-output" ratio	Branch and type of industry		"Working capital-output" ratio
Flour milling	A	0.09	Textile	A	0.31
	B	0.16		B	0.33
Production of vegetable oils	A	0.13	Footwear	A	0.19
	B	0.06		B	0.30
Soap making	A	0.29	Leather	A	0.41
	B	0.14		B	0.18
Chemical	A	0.40	Chemical	A	0.38
	B	0.29		B	0.13
General machine-building	A	0.41	Glass, ceramics	A	0.34
	B	0.34		B	0.54
Light machine-building	A	0.23	Goods made of cement and concrete	A	0.52
	B	0.16		B	0.56
Production of electrical goods	A	0.43	Metal goods	A	0.33
	B	0.17		B	0.21
Metallurgical	A	0.39	Machine-building	A	0.30
	B	0.22		B	0.52
Food	A	0.18	Production of plastics	A	0.32
	B	0.04		B	0.22

Compiled on the basis of data in Tables 3 and 4.

at enterprises in small-scale industry, i.e., in these branches, the situation does not favor small-scale industry.

The "working capital-output" ratio characterizes small-scale production from yet another side: even though, as a rule, the amount of working capital as compared with the mass of fixed capital is greater in small-scale production than in factory production, in a number of cases the amount of this capital per unit of output may be more "economical" specifically in small-scale production. Thus, if it is necessary to maximize output in the case of a shortage of capital, from among the various technological modes of production it is possible to select a variant that is optimal from the point of view of

outlays of both fixed and working capital.

Sometimes there may also arise a situation in which small-scale production is not entirely advantageous owing to a high "capital-output" index precisely because the amount of working capital per unit of output is high. Under these conditions, it is particularly useful to analyze capital-output ratio separately for fixed and working capital. Because it is easier to find ways of curtailing outlays of working capital per unit of output than of fixed capital, in certain cases this separate analysis can point the way to reducing production costs.

In planning investments, however, the "working capital-output" ratio index must be used with great caution and only after it has been verified whether working capital contains all the elements of this capital used by the enterprise. In a number of cases, the smaller size of this ratio in small-scale industry as compared with factory industry can also be explained by the fact that part of the working capital of small enterprises is in the hands of traders or master-middlemen who supply the craftsman or owner of a small manufacture with raw materials, cover sales costs, etc. Sometimes this unconsidered portion of the working capital can be very high, and this completely changes the picture of the capital structure of small enterprises. As noted above, the supplying of raw materials and "care" for the sale of finished goods constitute one of the principal methods used by the middlemen and money-lenders to enslave small commodity producers. Naturally, as a result of this, there is a decrease in the number of elements that form the small enterprise's working capital — for example, raw material stocks and finished output in the warehouses. As noted in the study of small-scale industry in Moradabad, "No fewer than 70% of the enterprises have small working capital. These enterprises are forced to process raw materials and semifinished goods belonging to others and to simply work for them for a wage. The sale of their output depends on orders placed with them by the middleman or merchant . . . . " (6)

Working capital of small enterprises consists of the following basic parts: stocks of raw materials, finished output in warehouses, incomplete production, and liquid assets. Raw materials account for 13.7-64.2% of all working capital. In most branches, however, this share constitutes one-fifth to one-fourth of all working capital. The share of finished output fluctuates from 7.5% (metallurgical) to 44.1% (leather industry). It should be noted that in a number of branches — flour milling, vegetable oil production, soap making, metallurgical, and general machine-building — the share of finished output in working capital is extremely low: in the range of 7.5-12.8%. The share of incomplete production is relatively low, particularly in such branches as vegetable oil production (0.9%),

soap making (5.5%), metallurgical (4.6%), and electrical commodity production (7.4%). (7)

Liquid assets include cash on hand [kassovaia nalichnost'], bank deposits, issued loans and advances, and accounts receivable. Cash on hand and bank deposits constitute a highly diverse share in various branches. In a number of branches, their share is low, e.g., in the flour milling (4.3%) and leather (3.7%) branches. In other branches, they occupy a considerable place in the working capital of enterprises, e.g., in the production of vegetable oils — 27.5%, in soap making — 11.7%; in metallurgy — 14.1%, etc. Data from the study in Moradabad confirm the high share of cash on hand and bank deposits in the working capital of small enterprises. As a whole, for all branches in the small-scale industry of Moradabad, these items accounted for 38.7% of working capital. In the group of branches in the metalworking industry, cash on hand and deposits accounted for 48.9% of all working capital. Baljit Singh, director of the study in Moradabad, explains this by the considerable use of hired labor at these enterprises. (8)

According to data at a survey in Delhi, accounts receivable are a very peculiar item in the working capital of small enterprises. They account for from 7.4% (leather industry) to 60.1% of working capital (metallurgical industry). According to the calculations of P. N. Dhar, throughout all branches as a whole, over 32% of working capital is accounted for by this item. Small enterprises that themselves are suffering from a shortage of credit have to extend credit to their customers on a broad scale. This practice is particularly widespread if the enterprise fills orders for local organs of authority (the printing industry). (9)

Comparison of the structure of the working capital of small-scale and factory production reveals that the share of raw material stocks is approximately the same in the flour milling and leather industries. In all other branches shown in Table 3, the share of raw material stocks is 2-3 times less in small-scale industry than in factory industry. (10) In the majority of branches, the share of finished output is also higher in the factory industry. The leather industry and light machine-building constitute an exception. The share of unfinished production in the factory industry is relatively small — on the average for all branches, 9% of the working capital. It is still somewhat higher, however, than in small-scale industry enterprises. It is characteristic that in the data of the census on the large-scale industry there is a total dearth of any kind of information on accounts receivable (an asset item), whereas in small-scale industry accounts receivable occupy a large place.

Comparison of the structure of working capital in small-scale and factory industry shows that, with respect to the basic items, small-scale industry is in a more favorable position even though, in our opinion, its working capital as well increased excessively as a result of these items. Accounts receivable, which occupy such a large place in the working capital of small-scale industry, do not actually contribute to the description of the productive activities of small-scale enterprises but only emphasize particular features in the relations of these enterprises with the market.

On the whole, the amount of working capital at small enterprises must be higher than in the factory industry if only because of the less "economic" conditions of production, supply, and sales. By virtue of their activity, however, small enterprises sometimes can get along with less working capital than is necessary for similar factory enterprises. They are able to "economize" on working capital. This possibility results from the fact that small enterprises, at any rate many of them, produce their goods from the customer's material. In such a case, there is no necessity to keep part of the capital in the form of raw material stocks and stored finished output waiting to be sold. It can be assumed that a small enterprise producing goods in small lots can organize a system of orders more easily than a similar large-scale factory enterprise. The system of orders is the breathing space that, in a number of cases, permits the small producer to hold his ground and even withstand the competition of factory production.

Under the present conditions characterizing developing nonsocialist countries, the system of producing according to order usually represents a form of predatory exploitation of craft and manufacture by merchant-moneylender's capital and sometimes by large-scale industrial capital. The system of orders permits the merchant-moneylender's capital to continue to exploit small-scale production even under the conditions of capitalist competition and the dominance of monopolies in the sphere of industrial production. Frequently in this process the small commodity producer performs as a hired worker. Under other socioeconomic conditions, however — in particular under conditions of the predominant influence of the government sector in the sphere of industrial production — the system of orders for small, nonseries lots of goods can become one of the important forms of government protectionism and an instrument for using small-scale production in the interests of society as a whole.

Labor Productivity

The following indices have been selected for the comparison of labor productivity in small-scale and factory industry: the amount of processed raw materials per worker, the gross output per worker, the net product (value added) per worker, the same indices per unit of wages paid out.

The first three indices give an idea of the level of labor productivity in two types of industrial production in a single country. The same group of indices in terms of the unit of wages paid out makes it possible to compare labor productivity in homogeneous branches of industry in various countries.

Data for the analysis are concentrated in Table 7 for a group of economically underdeveloped countries (India, Burma, Pakistan) and for one developed capitalist country (Japan). (11)

Let us examine the first group of indices. The greatest gap between labor productivity of workers in small-scale and factory industry is seen in India. As noted above, India's manufacturing industry is characterized by a combination of

Output

Branches		India (rupees)						Burma	
		R/N	P/N	y/N	R/V	P/V	y/V	R/N	P/N
Average for all branches	A	–	–	–	–	–	–	2,636	5,562
	B	–	–	–	–	–	–	840	1,704
Food	A	47,500	53,700	4,300	36.3	41.0	3.3	3,687	5,626
	B	5,600	7,400	1,230	7.9	10.5	1.7	1,341	2,565
Tobacco	A	–	–	–	–	–	–	857	1,772
	B	–	–	–	–	–	–	613	1,409
Textile	A	–	–	–	–	–	–	2,689	5,157
	B	–	–	–	–	–	–	1,003	1,698
Footwear	A	–	–	–	–	–	–	1,663	3,291
	B	–	–	–	–	–	–	776	1,717
Leather	A	–	–	–	–	–	–	9,527	12,085
	B	–	–	–	–	–	–	1,907	3,523
Woodworking	A	–	–	–	–	–	–	1,537	2,923
	B	–	–	–	–	–	–	288	719
Chemical	A	8,250	16,610	6,150	4.3	8.7	3.2	5,297	7,030
	B	960	3,950	1,340	1.7	7.2	2.4	1,921	2,925
Glass, ceramics	A	–	–	–	–	–	–	185	618
	B	–	–	–	–	–	–	156	910
General machine-building	A	4,850	8,100	3,040	3.1	5.2	2.0	268	1,259
	B	2,320	4,700	1,730	2.0	4.2	1.5	338	1,081
Metal goods	A	–	–	–	–	–	–	2,156	3,779
	B	–	–	–	–	–	–	597	1,459
Metallurgical	A	5,680	14,200	5,210	2.3	5.8	2.1	1,827	3,173
	B	380	1,360	765	0.5	1.9	1.1	500	1,484
Production of plastics	A	–	–	–	–	–	–	–	–
	B	–	–	–	–	–	–	–	–
Electrical goods	A	5,100	9,050	3,200	2.9	5.2	1.8	–	–
	B	5,350	8,650	2,590	3.4	5.5	1.6	–	–
Light machine-building	A	5,000	11,000	5,460	1.7	3.6	1.8	–	–
	B	1,920	3,600	1,210	2.3	4.4	1.5	–	–

Note. R–value of processed raw material; P–gross output; y–net product; N–number employed; V–

Sources: For India, Burma, and Pakistan—data from Tables 3-5; for Japan—Tiuse kige tokei eran

33

Table 7

Small-Scale (B) Industry in Certain Asian Countries

				Output							
(kyats)				Pakistan (rupees)						Japan (thousands of yen)	
y/N	R/V	P/V	y/V	R/N	P/N	y/N	R/V	P/V	y/V	y/N	y/V
1,529	5.5	11.7	3.2	–	–	–	–	–	–	605.6	2.7
835	2.0	4.1	2.0	–	–	–	–	–	–	285.9	2.2
1,770	7.5	11.4	3.6	16,900	21,200	3,750	13.6	17.1	3.0	705.1	4.0
1,168	3.1	5.9	2.7	12,700	15,700	2,350	11.6	14.4	2.2	338.7	3.0
904	2.6	5.4	2.7	–	–	–	–	–	–	–	–
784	2.1	4.9	2.7	–	–	–	–	–	–	–	–
2,337	6.8	13.0	5.9	3,400	6,000	1,980	3.4	6.0	2.0	314.8	2.1
677	2.7	4.6	1.8	3,220	5,150	1,760	3.6	5.8	2.0	212.1	2.1
1,601	3.4	6.7	3.2	5,400	9,350	3,700	2.9	5.1	2.0	–	–
916	1.5	3.4	1.8	2,580	4,200	1,610	2.2	3.6	1.4	–	–
2,461	9.3	11.8	2.4	6,100	12,000	2,700	5.7	11.2	2.5	470.4	2.3
1,555	2.3	4.3	1.9	27,100	36,700	7,935	18.4	24.9	5.4	319.7	2.2
1,241	2.7	5.1	2.2	–	–	–	–	–	–	384.5	2.4
417	1.0	2.4	1.9	–	–	–	–	–	–	263.0	2.2
1,594	13.5	18.0	4.1	4,000	7,650	2,500	3.3	6.2	2.0	865.9	2.9
957	5.4	8.2	2.7	10,850	16,200	2,200	7.6	11.3	1.5	531.2	3.0
425	1.0	3.2	2.2	1,010	2,900	1,050	1.2	3.5	1.2	622.5	2.7
745	0.3	2.0	1.6	1,960	3,350	1,370	1.8	3.2	1.3	277.0	1.9
705	0.4	2.1	1.2	2,450	4,500	1,800	2.6	4.8	1.9	591.3	2.3
599	0.6	1.9	1.0	2,720	4,270	1,730	2.0	3.2	1.3	326.9	1.7
1,454	3.5	6.2	2.4	3,600	5,850	1,860	3.5	5.7	1.8	522.1	2.4
830	1.3	3.1	1.8	2,520	4,660	1,780	2.6	4.8	1.8	304.9	2.0
1,305	1.7	2.9	1.2	–	–	–	–	–	–	645.0	1.8
926	0.8	2.2	1.4	–	–	–	–	–	–	362.8	1.9
–	–	–	–	2,860	5,050	1,760	3.2	5.6	2.0	–	–
–	–	–	–	1,980	4,600	2,280	2.0	4.6	2.3	–	–
–	–	–	–	–	–	–	–	–	–	–	–
–	–	–	–	–	–	–	–	–	–	–	–
–	–	–	–	–	–	–	–	–	–	–	–
–	–	–	–	–	–	–	–	–	–	–	–

wages paid out.

1961 [Statistical Survey of Industry], Tokyo, 1961, pp. 44-52, 70-78, 96-104.

highly developed modern forms of factory industry on the one hand and the most backward, routine forms of production in small-scale industry, particularly at dispersed manufacture enterprises, on the other. In some branches, the gap in the amount of processed raw material is 14 times (metallurgy); 9 (food); 9.5 (chemical); in the production of the gross product — 10 (metallurgy); 8.4 (food), 4.6 (chemical); in the production of the net product — 7.5 (metallurgy), 3.5 (food), and 4.5 (chemical, light machine-building).

In Burma the disparity in labor productivity within a branch is somewhat less. The greatest disparity in productivity per worker is observed in leather production (5 times in terms of the amount of raw material processed, 3.4 in terms of gross product, and 1.6 in terms of net product) and in the woodworking industry (5.3 times in terms of the amount of raw material processed, 4.0 in terms of gross product, and 3.0 in terms of net product).

In Pakistan's manufacturing industry there is a still smaller gap in labor productivity per worker than in India [sic — Burma]. The greatest gap is in the footwear industry: 2.1 times in terms of the quantity of raw material processed, 2.2 in terms of gross product, and 2.3 in terms of net product. At the same time, in a number of branches, particularly in the leather and the chemical, the picture is reversed; there is a higher labor productivity with respect to all or some indices per worker in small-scale industry as compared with factory industry.

The Japanese manufacturing industry is distinguished by greater uniformity with respect to the given indicator. Here, the maximum gap in the size of the net product per worker is 2.7 times (glass, ceramics), while the minimum gap is 1.5 times (textile industry). In our opinion, the explanation for this is to be sought in the comparatively higher degree of technical equipment in Japan's small-scale industry and in the higher organic composition of capital in it as compared with economically underdeveloped countries. In addition, Japan's small-scale industry is characterized by closer ties with the factory (12) than is the case in the aforemen-tioned developing countries, owing to which a certain leveling of the volume of output per worker is possible.

A second group of indices per unit of wages paid out adds to the picture. In addition to the great convenience that this system of indices provides — specifically the possibility of comparing international labor productivity — it also has basic importance in that it demonstrates the output of the gross and net product per unit of wages paid out. This is all the more important in view of the fact that the wage fund is a limiting factor in the developing countries.

Indices per unit of wages paid out level out differences in the output per worker in factory and small-scale industry. This is not surprising if we consider that in all of the countries investigated, not excluding Japan, the wages of the worker in small-scale industry are, as a rule, lower than in factory industry.

As can be seen in Table 7, in India the greatest gap for these indices is in the processing of raw materials and in gross output: 4.6 and 3.9 times, respectively, in the food industry, and 4.6 and 3.0 times in the metallurgical industry; in net output — 1.9 times (food, metallurgy). In Burma: raw materials processing — 4 times (leather) and 2.5 times (textile); in gross output — 2.8 times (textile), 2.7 (leather), 2.2 times (chemical); in net output — 3.3 times (textile). In Pakistan: in gross output — 1.4 (footwear) and in net output — 1.4 (footwear).

For the majority of branches of industry of economically underdeveloped countries cited in the table, however, the gap is much smaller than the "maximum" figures selected by us. Moreover, in certain branches of small-scale industry there is a higher productivity of labor per unit of wages. Thus, in Indian factory industry there is a larger gross output per worker in the electrical engineering industry and in light machine-building, while gross output per unit of wages paid out is smaller than in small-scale industry. A similar picture exists for net output in the production of plastics in Pakistan.

In developed capitalist Japan, the evening out of levels of productivity in small-scale and factory industry in terms of the index of output per unit of wages paid out is still more pronounced than in the developing countries. In net output, the gap between labor productivity in the two types of industrial production reaches its highest point in the glass-ceramics (2 times) and in the printing (1.4 times) industries. In the other branches, the gap in terms of net output is either still less or disappears completely or appears but is in favor of small-scale industry (chemical, metallurgical branches). Even in these two branches, however, the output per worker is, respectively, 1.6 and 1.8 times higher in the factory industry. The possibility is not excluded that this peculiarity, characteristic of Japan's manufacturing industry, is, together with other "merits" of small-scale production, that factor that additionally stimulates Japanese factory production toward symbiosis with small-scale production, to the subordination of it, and even to the development and expansion of it under the aegis of factory production. The leveling of the differences in output per unit of wages paid out is a very substantial factor for the capitalist entrepreneur in developing countries as well and, together with other factors, such as low capital-output ratio and others, unquestionably promotes the preservation and even a certain development of small-scale production.

It is known that the low level of earnings in the factory industry of developing countries results from a number of historical causes, especially the insufficient development of productive forces in general and of industry in particular, vast disguised and overt unemployment, pressure from the "surplus" labor force, and the relative weakness and lack of organization of the working class. In the course of economic development, as industry and the demand for skilled and semiskilled cadres grow and the power and organization of the factory proletariat increase, the wages of factory workers will unquestionably grow. At the same time, owing to the very conditions and organization of production (dispersion, lack of political organization of craftsmen and workers in small manufactures, factory competition in the internal market, etc.), the wages of workers in small-scale industry will remain at the previous level or will grow

extremely slowly and sporadically at times of the most favorable market conditions. Because the given indicator is directly proportional to the absolute indicator of output per worker and inversely proportional to the amount of wages received by the worker ($p = P/V$), an increase in the wage level in the factory industry in the face of a practically constant level of wage payments in small-scale industry tends to reduce the gap in this index between large-scale factory and small-scale industry. Modernization and rationalization of small-scale production itself — i.e., the factor increasing the absolute labor productivity — operate in a similar fashion.

It is difficult to say which tendency will prove to be more powerful: whether there will be a more rapid rise in the absolute labor productivity, or output per worker, in the factory industry and, as a result of this, a greater gap both in the absolute and relative (per unit of wages paid out) labor productivity in small-scale and factory industry of developing countries, or whether, on the other hand, factors reducing this gap will prove to be more powerful: a certain degree of technical progress and growth of labor productivity in small-scale industry, higher wages for factory workers while the wages of workers at small enterprises remain the same, etc. Evidently, owing to various economic and technical conditions, developing countries will be differentiated in this respect. In the first case, small-scale industry will be forced out by large-scale industry, as will handicraft production by factory production; in the second case, small-scale production will be subordinated to modern industry and will be widely used by large-scale industrial capital; under the aegis of the factory even its extensive development will be seen. Of course, this alternative will exist only until such time as there is (if this is altogether possible for one or another specific country) a complete or virtually complete absorption of the surplus labor force by large-scale industry and conditions are created for the elimination of the small-scale production by the large-scale, a feature that is characteristic of developed capitalist society.

We can draw certain general conclusions from the above comparison of labor productivity in the factory and small-scale industry:

1. The difference between them with respect to absolute labor productivity, or in terms of output per worker, is relatively great in developing countries, particularly where small-scale production is most backward and routine and is founded on antediluvian, traditional methods. Under the conditions of a normally functioning, developed economic system, the use of manpower resources in such unproductive forms is unquestionably wasteful. Therefore, the question of their existence on any considerable scale can only be within some limited transitional period when use is still made of factors and criteria other than the absolute productivity per worker.

2. Differences between the two types of industrial production with respect to labor productivity expressed in output per unit of wages paid out are somewhat leveled out as compared with the absolute labor productivity (per worker). As noted above, this circumstance, which generally favors the preservation and expansion of small-scale industry in developing countries, is particularly favorable to large-scale production that wishes to subordinate small-scale commodity production and to exploit it under its aegis. The tendency toward a still greater leveling of these differences, and the establishment of an approximately uniform level of output per unit of wages paid out (with the retention of low capital-output ratio and low wages in small-scale industry), are also advantageous to large-scale industrial capital. Under these conditions, large-scale capital will unquestionably strive to transform the manufacture and craft into an external section of the factory.

3. One should not forget, however, that differences in output per unit of wages in the factory and small-scale industry, even though they are less than the differences in absolute labor productivity, nonetheless do exist at the present time. This circumstance is very disadvantageous for small-scale production, particularly when the wage fund is the same basic restriction as productive capital. If these differences are very great, large-scale capital can simply refuse to participate in such activity, or it can consign small-scale production to its own fate, or even crush it with competition. Naturally, in solving the problem of the expediency and prospects for the existence of small-scale commodity production and the use of it in the interests of the national economy, the government cannot be guided by such calculations. In this case, the very question as to the expenditure of the wage fund, and of defining the size and limits of use of variable capital in modern and small-scale industry, becomes a subject of government policy. To put it more simply, if the wage fund is markedly limited, and the output per unit of wages is also to a considerable extent not to the benefit of small-scale production, then the government must solve the question of small-scale production on the basis of the aggregate of all other factors. First of all, it should be determined whether the government can provide a wage fund and use it optimally among already selected objects according to other, more important criteria (whether factory enterprises or enterprises of small-scale industry within some branch are selected according to these criteria). It seems to us that this is the way things stand in the majority of the presently developing countries.

Footnotes

1) For the sake of generalized comparison, small-scale industry is taken as a whole within those boundaries that are established by the official statistics of the investigated countries, abstracting from various types of enterprises. Similarly, corresponding branches in the factory industry are not broken down according to the size of enterprises.

2) "Report on Small-Scale Manufacture," The National Sample Survey, No. 19, Delhi, 1959, p. 16; "Report on the Sample Survey of Manufacturing Industries, 1951," The National Sample Survey, No. 15, Delhi, 1958, p. 47.

3) Baljit Singh, The Economics of Small-Scale Industries, pp. 38-39.

4) Ibid., p. 37.

5) K. Marx and F. Engels, Soch. Vol. 24, p. p. 186 (italics — S. K.).

6) Singh, op. cit., p. 37.

7) Here and subsequently, unless specifically stated otherwise, data on the structure of working capital are taken from P. D. Dhar, Small-Scale Industries in Delhi, p. 32.

8) Singh, op. cit., pp. 41-43.

9) Dhar, op. cit., p. 4.

10) Ibid., p. 32; Thirteenth Census of Indian Manufactures 1958 (Summary Report), Calcutta, 1960, pp. 22-33.

11) For Japan, there are data only on the net product.

12) J. Fei and G. Ranis, Innovation, Capital Accumulation, and Economic Development, New Haven, 1963, p. 301.

CHAPTER III

Comparison of Other Basic Indicators of the Productive Activity of Small-Scale and Factory Industry

The "Gross Output-Capital" Ratio

This ratio is one of the most important for comparing the effectiveness of small-scale and factory industry types of industrial production — types that differ in the degree of capital-intensiveness and in their role in the country's social reproduction. In determining the size of capital investments, both for the individual entrepreneur and for the government, of paramount importance is the profitability of these investments, i.e., the size of the surplus product. At the same time, from the point of view of social reproduction at a given historical moment, this division of the product into necessary and surplus product is temporarily obscured and the size of the product in its physical form becomes the most important factor. If, for example, 1,000 machine tools are required at a given time for the needs of social reproduction, the most important problem is that of producing precisely this quantity of machine tools by the least burdensome means from the point of view of capital outlays rather than the problem of what number of machine tools of those produced will embody the necessary labor and what number will embody the surplus labor. Unquestionably, in determining the volume of capital investments, it is necessary to consider both the problems of expanding production as well as the needs of social reproduction dictated by the moment.

Statistical data show that for the majority of the basic branches of the manufacturing industry of India, Burma, and Pakistan, the "gross output-capital" ratio is most favorable in small-scale industry (see Tables 3, 4, 5). For India, the coefficient P/K denoting this ratio, or the size of the gross output per unit of capital, in small enterprises engaged in the production of vegetable oils exceeds the corresponding indicator for large-scale industry by more than 2-5 [sic — 2.5] times; in soap making — 2.6 times; in the chemical industry — 65%; in the production of electrical commodities — 2.3 times; in the metallurgical industry — 3.3 times; in light machine-building — 1.8 times; etc. There are also exceptions: thus, in the flour milling industry, the coefficient P/K is higher for factory enterprises as compared with enterprises in small-scale industy.

In the manufacturing industry of Pakistan, owing to the above-mentioned greater capital-intensiveness of small-scale industry as compared with that of Indian industry (we are speaking, though, only of the city of Karachi), the gap in the size of coefficient P/K for small-scale and factory industry in general is not as considerable as in India's manufacturing industry. Here too the general trend can be seen rather clearly: for the majority of branches in Pakistan's manufacturing industry, the coefficient

38

P/K is higher in small-scale industry. The greatest differences in the dimensions of this indicator are seen in the food, chemical, glass, and ceramic branches of the manufacturing industry. In a number of branches — in the silk weaving, footwear industry, in machine-building — the "gross output-capital" ratio is higher at enterprises in the factory industry. Small enterprises in the silk weaving and machine-building industry have exceptionally high capital per worker. It is entirely natural, therefore, to assume that with respect to the basic indicators of their activity, these enterprises are extremely close to the factory enterprises.

The majority of the other materials on India and Pakistan also confirm the fact that, as a rule, the "gross output-capital" ratio is higher in small-scale industry. Thus, according to the data of a survey of the cotton weaving industry in the state of Bombay, the "gross output-capital" (fixed) ratio for factory and small-scale industry was 9.2:1 for the former and 14.5:1 for the latter; i.e., in small-scale industry, the gross output per unit of capital exceeded the corresponding indicator for the factory enterprises by more than 50%. (1)

For Burma, data are available only on fixed capital; the "gross output-capital" indicator is therefore calculated per unit of active fixed capital. On the whole, throughout the manufacturing industry of Burma, this indicator is higher at small enterprises (5.96:1 in small-scale industry as opposed to 5.02:1 in the factory industry). It can be seen that differences in the capital-output ratio in Burmese industry as a whole are not so considerable. Yet, in selecting from several technological modes of production, a large role is naturally played not only by the existence of differences among these modes with respect to one or another feature, but also by the degree of these differences. If the differences are small, any comparison or selection with respect to a given feature naturally loses its sense.

By no means, however, does the "gross output-capital" indicator favor small industry in all branches of Burma's manufacturing industry. In 7 out of 17 basic branches, this indicator is higher in the factory industry. Large fluctuations are also observed in those 10 branches in which this ratio is more favorable for small industry. Thus the gap in the volume of gross output per unit of capital is greatest in the textile and woodworking industry (approximately by 2.5 times) and in the production of petroleum products and coke (by 3.2 times); in the other branches the gap is 1.2-1.5 times. (2)

These data are evidence of the need for a differentiated approach to various branches when it is a matter of choosing from among one or another technological mode of production. Clearly, there is no selection problem when the factory production in some branch surpasses small-scale production in all basic indicators, including the "gross output-capital" indicator.

Data on the textile industry of Ceylon show how much capital must be invested to produce 500,000 yards of textiles under various technological modes of production (in thousands of rupees): (3)

Automatic looms (large factories)	485
Looms with mechanical engine (small factories)	262
Handlooms	78.5

Thus, the capital-output ratio at mills in Ceylon's textile industry is 1.8 times higher than in the small enterprises, and 6.2 times higher than in handicraft enterprises.

For some groups of enterprises in small-scale industry, the "gross output-capital" ratio may be unfavorable, i.e., lower than for factory enterprises in the same branch. It must be borne in mind, however, that in the given instance it is necessary to compare precisely heterogeneous enterprises. Otherwise one will run into errors.

In 1961, the Indian scientist P. Dhar and the American H. Lydall published a book containing sharp polemic material directed against proponents of developing small-scale industry. The authors noted that under the conditions of a weak and one-sidedly developed economy, in the evaluation of the effectiveness of capital investment, paramount importance is attached not only to the size of the surplus product anticipated from the capital investments but also to the size of the net product, including both surplus value and variable capital. In our view, the authors even somewhat exaggerate the significance of this factor. "...on the whole," they write, "the number one problem for the underdeveloped economy is the maximization of output." (4) Further, they cite data to show that the "net output-capital" ratio is higher at large enterprises than at small enterprises. Thus, in the textile industry this ratio increases from 0.24 to 0.63 in proportion to the growth of the size of the enterprises (in terms of the number of workers). A similar picture prevails in the other branches. Here, however, the authors are undoubtedly committing an error of a methodological type. The point is that Dhar and Lydall are taking enterprises of the same type, specifically the "large-scale" factory enterprises differing from one another only in the number of workers employed (from 20-49 to 500 and more workers). It is clear that within the group of large-scale enterprises, owing to a number of factors (large overhead expenses, etc.), the "output-capital" ratio can be particularly unfavorable precisely for the smaller enterprises with basically the same capital-output ratio as the other enterprises in this group. Other data used by Dhar and Lydall to prove that the output per unit of capital is higher in the factory industry are also not without shortcomings. For example, data on groups of enterprises working a different number of shifts, etc., cannot be compared. (5)

The selection of only some one group of enterprises in small-scale industry for comparison against factory industry can also lead to an erroneous conclusion. This can be seen in research by the Indian economist R. Balakrishna. For the purpose of comparison on the basis of the "output-capital" indicator, the author takes data on the nature of capital and output in only one branch — the paper industry. On the basis of the fact that this ratio is unfavorable for small-scale enterprises in this branch, Balakrishna makes the following general conclusion: "This shows that the 'capital-output' ratio in the unorganized sector is twice as high as in the organized (factory industry — S. K.). One can

imagine the enormous burden that the government and consumer must bear in supporting enterprises that are unable to compete." Further, R. Balakrishna is forced to admit that small-scale enterprises in a number of other branches do not come under this conclusion. (6)

The "gross output-capital" ratio may be different for groups of enterprises that differ in the size of capital investments or in employment within small-scale industry itself. The most complete data on this point are contained in the survey of small-scale industry in Moradabad. Small enterprises in Moradabad were classified in four groups according to the number employed: 2-4, 5-9, 10-14, 15-19 workers. The most advantageous "gross output-capital" ratio was seen in two average groups of enterprises with 5-9 and 10-14 workers. On the average, the fixed capital of these enterprises was 3,500 to 4,000 rupees; total invested capital was 4,800 rupees, and the invested capital of the smallest enterprises (2-4 workers) was, on the average, 1,500 rupees per enterprise. Enterprises with the lowest technical composition of capital were least advantageous from the point of view of gross output out of all groups of small enterprises. It should be noted, however, that even in them, as a rule, the "gross output-capital" ratio was higher than at enterprises in the factory industry. In the group of enterprises employing 15-19 persons, with a marked growth in investment capital (on the average to 25,000 rupees) we see a simultaneous drop in the size of gross output per unit of capital. (7) Thus for the branches selected in Moradabad, (8) maximum gross output per unit of invested capital was obtained at enterprises employing 5-14 workers and having a capital ranging between 4,000 and 8,000 rupees. Naturally, for other branches this maximum may be within other limits.

When assessing the importance of such an indicator as the "gross output-capital" ratio, for comparing the effectiveness of capital investments in various technological modes, it should be borne in mind that during a certain transition period, in proportion to the increase in capital per worker in the factory industry, the gap in the capital-output ratio between factory industry and small-scale industry will inevitably increase, i.e., the "output-capital" indicator during a given period will become more and more favorable to small-scale industry. Unquestionably a certain growth in capital per worker will occur in small-scale industry as well; but, as the data show, the technical retooling of small-scale production, if it takes place at all, will proceed at a much slower pace than in the factory industry. Thus, the transition period in developing countries is characterized by a relative (compared with small-scale industry) growth of the capital-output ratio in modern forms of industrial production.

Attention should be paid to still another circumstance that is connected with the capital-output ratio. All figures we have examined up to now characterize the productive effectiveness of capital investments already realized (mastered and in operation). Yet the "gross output-capital" coefficient (like other indicators) is not uniform at first, when the capital investments are only being mastered, and for several years thereafter, when the capital has been completely mastered and put into operation and has already been depreciated in part. We find some data on this point in the book by the Indian economist V. V. Bhatt: "If we assume that on the average the period of realization of capital investments continues for two years — i.e., investments made in a given year yield output only in the third year — then the average "capital-output" ratio will be 3.4:1 during the first 5 years, 2.6:1 in the first 10 years, and 2.4:1 during the first 15 years. For the 12-to-15 year period, the "capital-output" ratio will therefore be approximately 2.5:1." (9)

Thus, in evaluating the capital-output ratio of one or another technological mode, it is necessary to isolate the capital-output ratio during the initial period of production (10) and the capital-output ratio when the production has already been organized and the capital investments realized (or the "operational" effect of capital investments). It is clear that the "incremental" and "operational" effects refer not only to the "gross output-capital" ratio but also to other indicators of investment effectiveness — to the "net output-capital" ratio, to the surplus value norm, and to the profit norm. The period of investment realization, during which the capital-output ratio of production is inevitably higher, differs for various branches and technological modes of production. Evidently, the duration of this period can only be determined empirically. Further, the dimensions of the capital-output ratio during the "incremental" period differ for various countries. By way of illustration, we shall cite UN data on the magnitude of the generalized capital-output ratio during the initial period of capital investments in a number of Asian countries. The materials cited represent the average indicator for 1950-1959: (11)

"Capital-output" ratio during the period of realization

India	4.8
Burma	3.4
Pakistan	3.0
Thailand	2.6
Ceylon	2.9
Philippines	1.2
Indonesia	1.7

The above data on India differ somewhat from Bhatt's data. This is probably explained by the fact that the UN materials make use of the indicators of gross capital investment that overstate the amount of capital per unit of output. Nonetheless, in our view the overall trend is correctly reflected. The capital output during the period of realization is very high. The compilers explain this on the basis of two fundamental reasons: the underutilization of part of the fixed capital and the high degree of capital-intensiveness in new projects. (12)

The extremely low level of the capital-output ratio in the Philippines and Indonesia chiefly results from the fact that new capital investments in this period have been mainly expended on the restoration of industrial units destroyed by the war, which with relatively small capital investments has yielded a considerable increase in output. (13) In our opinion, in addition to fac-

42

tors relating to business conditions, it is possible to isolate several stable factors that determine differences in the magnitude of the "incremental" effect of capital investments. Among these are differences in the branch structure of industrial investments, the use of technological modes that differ in terms of the degree of capital-intensiveness, the rate at which new capacities are put into operation, the degree to which investments are mastered, etc.

How will this difference affect the determination of effectiveness of capital investments?

Here a twofold approach can be worked out. If the plan is for capital investments from which it is important to obtain an effect within a short period of time, primary emphasis must be placed on the capital-output ratio indicator during the period when the investments are put into operation. The longer the period for which the capital investments are calculated, the greater is the significance of the capital-output ratio indicator in the subsequent period. According to Bhatt's data, in the case of capital investments calculated for 15 years or more, the "incremental" effect can practically be neglected or slight adjustments can be made in the corresponding "operational" indicator.

Comparison of the "incremental" effect under various technological modes of production introduces additional characteristics to the indicator of capital investment effectiveness. If the capital investments are calculated for a short period (let us say, for 5-10 years), the most favorable position will be occupied by the less capital-intensive units having less marked differences between "incremental" and "operational" effects. Unquestionably, in short-term investment planning this is one more argument in favor of small-scale industry with a low level of mechanization.

As a general conclusion, let us note that: (1) on the whole, small-scale production is characterized by a higher "gross output-capital" ratio than factory industry; (2) the disparity in the capital-output ratio between these two basic types of production is particularly great in the initial period, i.e., during the period when the investments are being put into operation; and

(3) in addition to choosing between the aforementioned two types of production on the basis of larger output per unit of capital, it is possible to increase output further by using optimal technological modes within small-scale production.

Value Added, Surplus Product, Profit

We shall examine the following indicators: (1) the "value added-capital" ratio, or the sum of income per unit of capital investment (y/K); (2) the "surplus value-variable capital" ratio, or exploitation norm (m/V); and (3) the "surplus value-capital" ratio, or the profit norm (m/K).

The sum of income per unit of capital investment is an indicator that carries a double load. On the one hand, it characterizes the real level of employment that a unit of capital investment provides — naturally, with a given and averaged level of labor costs. On the other hand, it can be used as the further development of the "output-capital" indicator, but in a more refined form. The value of the product in this case is cleansed of the magnitude of the transferred value [perevesennaia stoimost'].

According to the data in Table 3, the "value added-capital" ratio in India's manufacturing industry is higher in small enterprises. In certain branches, the difference is very considerable, e.g., in the production of vegetable oils, electrical goods, and metallurgy.

Baljit Singh, the director of the Moradabad study, also arrives at the conclusion as to the more favorable "net output-capital" ratio, in a number of cases, in the small-scale and cottage industry: "There is considerable evidence to indicate that the net output per unit of investment in the small-scale sector is two to three times as high as in the large-scale industries ...however, this general conclusion does not extend to very small enterprises and household production units. In this case, there is also a saving of capital even though it is not as great." (14)

In Pakistan's manufacturing industry, the difference in the given coefficient between small-scale and factory production is not as great as in India. As already noted, this is explained by particular features in the very structure of small-scale Pakistani industry. Nonetheless, here, too, in the majority of branches this ratio is in favor of small-scale production. The silk weaving, footwear, and machine-building industries are exceptions.

In Burma's industry, the "net output-capital" (fixed) ratio on the whole is also in favor of small-scale production, even though the reverse is true in a number of branches. Thus, if one takes the data we used for 17 basic branches in Burma's manufacturing industry (Table 5), in 11 of them this ratio is higher for small-scale production and in 6 of them it is higher for factory production.

The disparity in the magnitude of the "net output-capital" ratio or of income per unit of capital investment in small-scale and factory industry increases as a function of differences in the degree to which they are mechanized. Indeed, in India's manufacturing industry, where differences in the level of technical equipment of small-scale and factory industry are greatest, differences in the dimensions of value added per unit of capital investment are also particularly noticeable. Thus, the sum of the fixed capital per worker in the production of vegetable oils for factory and small-scale industry is 2,720 and 435 rupees, respectively. Coefficient y/K is 0.26 and 0.88; in the production of electrical goods — 2,430 and 1,100 rupees and 0.51, 1.00, respectively, etc.

In Pakistan where, according to the data we used (Karachi), differences in fixed capital per worker in small-scale and factory industry are not as great, there is also considerably less difference in the dimensions of the value added per unit of capital. In the food industry, the sum of fixed capital per worker is 4,500 and 2,500 rupees, and coefficient y/K is 0.45 and 0.74; in the textile industry — 4,150 and 3,120 rupees and 0.33, 0.36; in the chemical industry — 6,800 and 2,870 rupees and 0.26, 0.44, etc.

The data cited on the Indian textile industry, with a more detailed breakdown as to various

technological modes than data used by us, still more convincingly confirm the fact that the highest dimensions of value added per unit of invested capital are observed specifically in the less mechanized production units (see table below). (15)

(rupees)

Technological mode	Value added per unit of fixed capital	Value added per worker
Handloom with flying shuttle	9.0	450
Semiautomatic handloom	7.5	1,500
Domestic mechanical loom	1.5	2,250
Factory mechanical loom	1.5	6,000
Automatic loom	0.6	48,000

Under conditions characterizing the present economy of a number of developing countries (we emphasize, specifically under these conditions), industry with a low level of mechanization has certain reserves, such as relatively high value added per unit of capital. Further, among various technological modes in small-scale industry it is possible to select a variant that is optimal in this respect.

How can it be explained that the net output per unit of capital investment is higher in small-scale industry in a number of cases? It seems to us that two important factors can be established:

1. The relatively low labor productivity at factory enterprises of developing countries, notwithstanding the development of modern technological modes in recent years. Indeed, as can be seen from the data cited, the growth of the technical base of factory enterprises as compared with small-scale enterprises is accompanied by a proportional increase in the size of the gross output, in the value of the processed raw material, or even in net output per worker.

2. The low cost of manpower, particularly in small-scale industry, that is characteristic of developing countries. For the "value added-capital" ratio, the significance of this is that in this case variable capital constitutes only a small part of the capital investments in the working capital of enterprises.

In small-scale industry, where a considerable part of the labor force is made up of "owners" of the enterprises and members of their families, the share of variable capital in all of the enterprise's capital altogether tends toward zero, because this part of the labor force receives remuneration only after the sale of finished output or subsists on usurer's credit, and these outlays are not reflected in capital expenditures. Accordingly, the sum of the enterprise's capital is artificially understated and coefficient y/K grows. The principal explanation of this phenomenon lies in the specific conditions characteristic for the economics of developing countries, in their general economic situation.

The aforementioned peculiarity of small-scale industry — higher income per unit of capital investment — on the one hand means large-scale employment for one and the same capital. For countries having "surplus" able-bodied population this circumstance unquestionably plays a large part. On the other hand, the higher "value added-capital" ratio means that at a given level of capital investment, more net output necessary for the needs of reproduction can be produced (16) and there is a greater possibility of providing reproduction with the necessary components.

It should be borne in mind, however, that the higher indicators of small-scale industry in the production of the gross and net product (where this is really the case) and the relative effectiveness (in terms of the given indicators) of substituting labor for capital have their limits. In the substitution of processes with a high capital-output ratio by labor-intensive processes there is a certain critical point below which not only the aforementioned advantage disappears but labor itself becomes entirely inexpedient. By way of an example, we can cite the well-known Indian experiment of introducing the manually operated spinning wheel in the interest of increasing employment — the "Ambar Charkha experiment."

As noted above, manual spinning is utterly unable to withstand the competition of factory production both in terms of the quality of the items as well as their cost. Most of the handicraft weavers in India, Pakistan, and other such countries chiefly use factory-made yarn. Nonetheless, in postwar India serious attempts have been made to revive this branch of handicraft production. The most enticing aspect of the Ambar Charkha experiment was the possibility of providing employment with very insignificant capital investments (a manually operated spinning wheel costs 100 rupees).

But what are the basic economic indicators of work with "Ambar Charkha"?

Production on a spinning wheel is unprofitable from beginning to end. The wages received by the worker absolutely do not provide the means of subsistence "even in such a poor country as India" (Sen). In order to "employ" a worker with the aid of the "Ambar Charkha" and to provide him with subsistence, an annual dole would be required. According to the very minimal estimates, this dole would be 138 rupees, 2 anna. The lowest wage limit is 9 anna, which the factory worker receives. While creating 30 rupees' worth of net product per worker per year, the "Ambar Charkha" simultaneously requires 4 times more nonproductive capital outlays. (17) Clearly, such manifestly inexpedient technical modes of production can also be found in other branches of small-scale industry.

As a rule, the mass of surplus product per worker is greater in the factory industry. The most significant differences with respect to this indicator are seen in India's industry. Thus in the metallurgical industry, the gap is almost 45 times; in light machine-building — more than 6 times, in the food industry — 5.5 times, etc. The gap is also great in certain branches of Burma's industry. In Pakistan's industry this gap is not greater than 2-2.5 times. In 5 out of 11 basic branches in the manufacturing industry of Pakistan, the amount of surplus value per worker in small-scale industry is higher than in the factory industry. A similar phenomenon is also observed in certain branches of Burma's manufacturing industry. Characteristically, the greater portion of the surplus value in small-scale production in a number of industrial branches in Pakistan and Burma is created with smaller investment of productive capital than in factory enterprises.

Similarly, the norm of surplus value, or the exploitation norm, is also higher in the factory industry of the developing countries. The ratio of the surplus product (18) to the annual wage fund is presented as a norm of surplus value. In calculating the annual wage fund in small-scale industry, we proceed from the wages of a hired worker in this industry.

In factory industry in India (see Table 3) the norm of surplus value fluctuates between 83% (light machine-building) and 407% (soap making industry); in small-scale industry — from 9% (metal casting) to 185% (soap making industry).

In Pakistan (see Table 4) the norm of surplus value fluctuates as follows: in the factory industry — from 25% (glass and ceramics industry) to 202% (food); in small-scale industry — from 29% to 156% (items made from cement and concrete). In the branch-by-branch comparison, the norm of surplus value in Pakistan's manufacturing industry is, as a rule, higher in factory production. In Pakistan, however, there are instances where the reverse is true, particularly in the leather and glass industries, in production of items made of cement, and in plastics.

In the overwhelming majority of branches in Burma's manufacturing industry, the surplus value norm is also higher in the factory production (see Table 5). On the whole, the surplus value norm for Burma's manufacturing industry is 222% in the factory industry as opposed to 99% in small-scale industry. For certain branches the difference is still greater. Thus in Burma's textile industry this norm is 490% in the factory industry as against 83% in small-scale industry. In the woodworking industry it is 116% as opposed to 40%, respectively, etc. Only in 2 branches out of 17 is the surplus value norm higher in small-scale industry — in the production of petroleum products and in metal-

lurgy. But in the latter instance, the norm of surplus value is very low in both factory and small-scale industry: 19% and 40%, respectively.

It is interesting to compare the norm of exploitation in the developing countries and in postwar Japan. On the whole, for Japan's manufacturing industry, the surplus value norm constitutes 170% in factory industry and 120% in small-scale industry. The highest exploitation norm is observed in the large-scale food industry, where it constitutes 298%. In the other branches, this norm is more or less close to the aforementioned average figures.

Unlike Japanese industry, in the industry of the investigated developing countries one can observe a great diversity in the size of the surplus value norm. Side by side with branches with an excessively high surplus value norm (in India, in the soap making industry — 407%; in Pakistan, at small enterprises in the leather industry — 440%, etc.), there are branches with an extremely low surplus value norm (see Tables 3 and 4).

How can such variety and diversity be explained? In our opinion, first by the fact that industry itself in these countries has not achieved any kind of homogeneity, and no single market of labor and capital has formed that would equalize differences in the conditions of exploitation of labor in individual branches and at enterprises of various types by the transfer of capital and manpower. This in turn can serve as an additional explanation of the viability of various forms of production in the developing countries, and of the persistent survival of what would seem to be the most unprofitable forms alongside modern industry.

In their own way, the generally higher surplus value per worker and the higher exploitation norm in the factory industry, as compared with small-scale industry, adjust the "abnormal" situation for the large-scale entrepreneur whereby small-scale industry has certain advantages over the factory industry with respect to the volume of gross output and newly created value per unit of capital; this provides a stimulus to build modern enterprises of the factory type.

46

As a rule, the profit norm in India's manufacturing industry is higher at factory enterprises. An exception to this is the production of vegetable oil, the chemical and pharmaceutical industry, and the production of the electrical goods in which the profit norm is higher at small-scale enterprises (see Table 3). The highest profit norm is in the soap making industry (58% at factory enterprises and 55% at small enterprises), while the lowest profit norm is in the metallurgical (14% at large-scale enterprises and 10% at small enterprises). On the whole, differences in the profit norm at factory and small enterprises in India's manufacturing industry are not very great. Strange as it may be, the greatest differences in the profit norm are seen precisely in those branches where this norm is most favorable for small-scale industry. Thus in the production of vegetable oils, the profit norm is 16% and 31% for large-scale and small-scale enterprises, respectively; 27% and 35% in the chemical industry; and 23% and 29% in the production of electrical goods.

Another situation holds true in the examined basic branches of Pakistan's manufacturing industry. Here the higher profit norm is found in small-scale industry in the majority of the branches. Only in the silk-weaving, footwear, and machine-building branches of industry is the profit norm higher at factory enterprises (see Table 4).

Differences in the profit norm between the two types of industry are also more considerable in Pakistan than in India. Thus, in Pakistan, according to the data we use, the profit norm for the factory and small-scale industry, respectively, is as follows: 30% and 39% in the food industry; 34% and 65% in the cotton industry; 21% and 2% in the silk-weaving industry; 57% and 24% in the footwear industry; 24% and 47% in light chemistry; 24% and 8% in machine-building, etc.

It is interesting to compare data on the profit norm, adduced by us from the Pakistan industrial census, with data from other sources. Thus, according to the calculations of Mahbub ul Hag, the head of the long-range planning department of the Pakistan Planning Commission, the aver-

age profit in the nation's factory industry is approximately 30%, [19] which is very close to the data cited above. Unquestionably, this profit norm is extremely high. All the more important is the fact that small enterprises in a number of industrial branches in Pakistan have a still higher profit norm. According to Sen's calculations, the profit norm in India's textile industry is higher for factory enterprises. However, at small enterprises of this industry as well, it is comparatively high (32%-39%). This is shown by the following data (in rupees). [20]

Technological mode	Fixed capital	Working capital	Total capital	Annual profit norm (%)
Handloom with flying shuttle	50	413	463	32
Semiautomatic handloom	200	1,350	1,550	39
Domestic mechanical loom	1,500	1,913	3,413	40
Factory mechanical loom	4,000	4,875	8,875	51
Automatic loom	10,000	4,547	14,547	40

As Sen's data show, within an individual branch there is a vast area for selecting the most effective technological mode, including selection on the basis of profit norm. Thus, in the given example an equal profit norm is yielded by investment in a domestic mechanical loom and in automatic factory equipment with an excessive capital-output ratio. The highest profit norm is realized not in the production with the highest capital-output ratio, but in the factory production unit with nonautomatic mechanical looms, where the capital-output ratio is lower. Finally, slightly improved manual equipment — semiautomatic handlooms — shows a slightly lower profit norm than mechanical equipment with an incomparably higher capital-output ratio.

But what are the basic factors that affect the profit norm in the industry of the countries investigated?

The basic profit norm formula

$$p' = \frac{m}{K} \qquad (1)$$

can also be written in the following form:

$$p' = \frac{m \cdot V}{V \cdot K} = m' \frac{V}{K}, \qquad (2)$$

where m' is the surplus value norm; K is the total utilized productive capital; and V is the cost of labor force. (21)

Provided that all capital is expended in one year, the V/K relationship designates the value structure of capital. In reality, however, a part of the permanent capital is expended in the course of a number of years. In this case, the relationship V/K cannot express the value structure of capital. Nonetheless, this relationship is directly linked to the structure of capital. Any change in the value structure of capital entails a change in V/K as well in the same direction. If it is assumed that the period of amortization of fixed capital is the same for various branches and enterprises (conditionally, ten years, according to the UN norm), an interbranch comparison according to the V/K coefficient can be made. Accordingly, for practical calculations we may use the relationship V/K, owing to its direct dependence on the value structure of capital as being to a greater or lesser extent an approximate expression of the latter. Because the profit norm itself is calculated with respect to the total invested capital, (22) in our view it is preferable to use this indicator rather than a direct expression of the value composition of capital.

Thus, Formula 2 expresses the dependence of the profit norm on two basic factors: the surplus value norm and the value structure of capital. (23) In our concrete case, the value composition of capital can be viewed as its organic structure because differences in the value structure of capital at enterprises in the factory and small-scale industry also reflect differences in the technical composition of capital. We can in passing observe that the higher the ratio V/K in

Formula 2, the lower is the organic structure of capital.

When making practical calculations according to Formula 2, considering the imperfections of available statistics and the actual great differences in the duration of capital turnover, difficulties in calculating the true cost of labor power, etc., it is also necessary to make the following allowances and assumptions:

Annual volume and corresponding norms are taken as the volume and norm of surplus value as well as the profit norm. This approach equalizes differences in capital turnover at enterprises and in branches.

The sum of wages paid out for a year is taken as the value of the labor power. Formula 2 is used below in the light of these assumptions.

The norm of surplus value and the organic composition of capital, which act as opposing factors in Formula 2 (the profit norm is directly proportional to the norm of surplus value and inversely proportional to the organic composition of capital), change irregularly in the process of historical development from the lowest to the highest form of production. The growth in the technical composition of capital and the increase in the available capital per worker (and this is precisely the aspect of the matter that interests us here) lead to the growth of the exploitation norm and to an increase in the organic composition of capital. Nonetheless, the growth of these two factors is not necessarily synchronous. First one, and then the other, factor may lag, thus causing spasmodic fluctuations in the profit norm. It is precisely this point that is illustrated by data on the profit norm in the industry of India and Pakistan.

In the investigated branches of India's industry, the organic composition of capital is everywhere higher at factory enterprises. This factor, however, which lowers the profit norm, in most branches is exceeded by a considerably higher surplus value norm at enterprises of the factory type as compared with small enterprises. Let us take two branches — flour milling and general machine-building — as examples. The indicators for factory and small-scale industry are designated by indices 1 and 2, respectively.

48

Flour milling industry:

$$m'_{(1)} = 2.30 \ (230\%); \qquad m'_{(2)} = 0.74 \ (74\%);$$
$$\frac{V_{(1)}}{K_{(1)}} = 0.143; \qquad \frac{V_{(2)}}{K_{(2)}} = 0.417;$$
$$P'_{(1)} = m'_{(1)}\frac{V_{(1)}}{K_{(1)}} = 0,33 \ (33\%). \quad P'_{(2)} = m'_{(2)}\frac{V_{(2)}}{K_{(2)}} = 0.31 \ (31\%).$$

General machine-building:

$$m'_{(1)} = 0.96 \ (96\%); \qquad m'_{(2)} = 0.53 \ (53\%):$$
$$\frac{V_{(1)}}{K_{(1)}} = 0.26; \qquad \frac{V_{(2)}}{K_{(2)}} = 0.44;$$
$$P'_{(1)} = m'_{(1)}\frac{V_{(1)}}{K_{(1)}} = 0.25 \ (25\%). \quad P'_{(2)} = m'_{(2)}\frac{V_{(2)}}{K_{(2)}} = 0.23 \ (23\%).$$

It should be noted that in all examples we are using, m = mn; V = Vn, where n is the number of capital turnovers per year.

Let us now examine those branches of India's industry that we consider exceptions in the given instance, because they constitute a minority and the profit norm in them is higher for small enterprises.

Chemical industry (including the pharmaceutical industry):

$$m'_{(1)} = 2.20 \ (220\%); \qquad m'_{(2)} = 1.43 \ (143\%);$$
$$\frac{V_{(1)}}{K_{(1)}} = 0.123; \qquad \frac{V_{(2)}}{K_{(2)}} = 0.248;$$
$$P'_{(1)} = m'_{(1)}\frac{V_{(1)}}{K_{(1)}} = 0.27 \ (27\%). \quad P'_{(2)} = m'_{(2)}\frac{V_{(2)}}{K_{(2)}} = 0.35 \ (35\%).$$

Here, as in other branches constituting an "exception," the growth of the organic composition of capital, which lowers the profit norm, is not accompanied by an adequate increase in the exploitation norm.

In Pakistan's manufacturing industry, the surplus value norm is higher for factory enterprises only in six out of ten basic branches. In four branches, this norm is higher for small enterprises. Even in branches where this norm is higher for factory enterprises, it does not so significantly exceed the surplus value norm in small-scale industry. At the same time, the organic composition of capital in all basic branches, excepting the leather branch, is lower

at small enterprises. This explains why the profit norm is higher at small and handicraft enterprises in the majority of the branches we investigated in Pakistan's manufacturing industry. At small enterprises in the leather industry, the organic composition of capital is higher than at factory enterprises. However, the profit norm in this branch as well is higher at small enterprises because the influence of the high organic composition of capital, which lowers the profit norm, is brought to naught by the extraordinarily high surplus value norm (440% against 152% at enterprises in the large-scale industry).

The fact that, in a number of branches of the manufacturing industry of India and particularly of Pakistan, the profit norm is higher at small enterprises is primarily linked to the "lag" in the surplus value norm behind the growth of the technical composition of capital in these branches. In turn, the "lag" of the surplus value norm is explained by a number of factors inherent in the very nature of the economics of developing countries. Among these factors, the very low wages of workers in small-scale industry must be mentioned. That the labor power in small-scale production is paid much less than its value can be seen if only in the fact that the small producer must, as a rule, make extensive use of the unpaid labor of members of the family in order to provide for the material needs of his family. In factory production, this situation is somewhat adjusted and wages approximate the value of the labor power, even though at factory enterprises as well, owing to the constant availability of "surplus" hands, the labor power is generally paid less than its value. Nonetheless, at the present time such a situation as prevails at small enterprises in the factory industry is no longer possible in the developing countries. The growing strength and political organization of the factory proletariat, and the existence and growth of the government sector at whose enterprises the working conditions are usually better than at privately owned enterprises, also have an indirect effect on the situation of the entire factory proletariat, etc. The wage level, which is lower in small-scale production than in the factory industry, "pulls" the surplus value norm in small-scale production up to the norm in the factory industry.

Among the other causes of the "lag" in the surplus value norm behind the growth in the organic structure of capital in the factory industry of developing countries we should also mention unquestionable shortcomings in the organization of the production process — shortcomings that are caused by the lack of a skilled labor power, managerial cadres, and engineering and technical personnel. Unquestionably, the not entirely rational system of production organization reduces the effectiveness of production and lowers the absolute volume of the surplus value produced, thus lowering the overall surplus value norm and hence the profit norm in the factory industry.

But what is the trend toward change in the profit norm in developing countries?

In terms of the profit norm, small enterprises can be divided into two groups. One group contains enterprises in which not only are such indicators as gross and net output of capital invested higher than in the factory industry, but the profit norm is also higher. The second group contains enterprises that, while in terms of a number of indicators are in more favorable circumstances than corresponding enterprises of the factory industry, are nonetheless inferior with respect to such an indicator as the profit norm.

Notwithstanding the fact that enterprises in the first group can hardly be called "exceptions" at the present time, particularly in Pakistan, where branches with a higher profit norm in small-scale industry are too numerous, in our opinion, the historical tendency is that in the course of economic development the factory industry will everywhere have a higher profit norm than small-scale industry. This assumption is based on the following considerations.

On the one hand, in the developing countries, the law of the tendency for the profit norm to decline cannot but hold; this is a general law that is manifested with growth in the organic composition of capital. As modern forms of production assume the dominant position in the internal

market of these countries, this law will be ever more clearly and discernibly expressed in the direct dependence of the profit norm on the organic composition of capital.

Further, at the present time, a number of factors that are inherent in industrially underdeveloped countries promote the particular profitability of industrial investments. In the first place, mention should be made of the very low degree of saturation of the internal market with industrial goods. This permits the local manufacturers to jack up prices artificially and thus, together with the representatives of commercial capital (and not infrequently commercial-industrial capital in these countries is combined in one firm), to exact an additional profit. As industrial production increases and the internal market becomes saturated with goods, such factors will unquestionably have less and less importance and the profit norm will decline to the usual level found in the developed countries.

But on the other hand, as Marx noted, the implementation of the law of the tendency for the profit norm to decline is fraught with a number of opposing factors that "weaken" and "paralyze" its effect even in developed capitalist society. (24) These factors can be all the more powerful in the transitional economies of developing countries.

One of these factors is the increase in the degree of labor exploitation. Intensified exploitation of the workers can be achieved both by the use of more productive equipment as well as by the organization of production that promotes the intensiveness of work. Further, a certain rise in wages in small-scale industry can be foreseen, particularly if the government involves itself in this matter. Of course, wages at small-scale and handicraft enterprises can hardly reach the level that is characteristic for large-scale factory enterprises. Nonetheless, as the small producer is liberated from the middlemen and moneylenders, there will unquestionably be a certain increase in wages. And this increase in wages will reduce the overall level of the profit norm at these enterprises and will therefore put the factory enterprises in a more

50

favorable position with respect to the profit norm as compared with small-scale enterprises. Even the tendency toward a decline in the profit norm, as a result of the decrease in speculative profit connected with the shortage of industrial goods, may remain only a tendency as the internal market becomes saturated with these goods. Naturally, in making calculations for a relatively short period of time, use can be made of the existing, already formed profit norm in one or another branch. In planning for a long period it is essential to make more complex calculations of possible changes in the profit norm, taking into account the factors discussed above.

Footnotes

1) "Report on the Census of Weaving Industry in Maharashtra State," Quarterly Bulletin of Economics and Statistics, Vol. I, No. 2, July-September 1960, p. 19.

2) Union of Burma, First Stage Census 1953, Vol. II, pp. 51-60 (see Table 5).

3) ILO. Report to the Government of Ceylon on the Development of a Textile Industry on a Decentralised Basis, Part II, Geneva, 1962, p. 23.

4) P. N. Dhar and H. F. Lydall, The Role of Small Enterprises in Indian Economic Development, p. 11.

5) Ibid., pp. 14-17.

6) R. Balakrishna, Review of Economic Growth in India, Bangalore, 1961, pp. 158-159.

7) Baljit Singh, The Economics of Small-Scale Industries, pp. 49-52.

8) Copper-smelting, the production of copper items, metal-carving and engraving, galvanic coating and other types of metalworking; food, leather, textile, woodworking enterprises; the paper industry, ceramics, etc. As can be seen, the range of branches selected for the given survey is rather broad.

9) V. V. Bhatt, Employment and Capital Formation in Underdeveloped Economies, Bombay, 1960, p. 76.

10) In our estimation, it can be defined by the expression "incremental" effect of capital investments, from the word "increment" — growth, increase. In foreign literature, the term "incremental" designates characteristics of one or another economic indicator during the period when the investments are being put into operation.

11) Economic Survey for Asia and the Far East, Bangkok, 1961, p. 24.

12) Ibid., p. 24.

13) Ibid.

14) Singh, op. cit., p. 53.

15) UN World Economic Survey 1961, Geneva, 1962, p. 54.

16) Here we are abstracting from the technical possibilities of one or another type of production in the manufacture of the necessary product. We conditionally assume that the basic products under discussion can be manufactured both by the factory and handicraft modes.

17) Report of the Ambar Charkha Enquiry Committee, Ministry of Production Government of India, 1956; A. K. Sen, Choice of Techniques. An Aspect of Theory of Planned Economic Development, Oxford, 1960, pp. 116-118.

18) Statistical data on developing countries make it possible to calculate the surplus product by subtracting the annual wage fund from the annual sum of the net product.

19) Mahbub ul Haq, The Strategy of Economic Planning. A Case Study of Pakistan, Karachi, 1963, p. 47.

20) Sen, op. cit., p. 112.

21) See K. Marx and F. Engels, Soch., Vol. 25, Part I, pp. 57-58, 62.

22) Ibid., pp. 50, 57-58.

23) Ibid., p. 78.

24) Ibid., p. 233.

CHAPTER IV

The Problem of "Capital-Intensive Versus Labor-Intensive Production" in the Works of Foreign Scholars

The economic indicators of the factory and small-scale industry examined earlier give us an idea of the complexity of the problem of choosing between these two types of industrial production under the conditions of the developing economies of former colonies and dependent countries.

Comparison of these indicators paints a very diverse and frequently contradictory picture. The most common case, however, is the one in which the more capital-intensive production also proves to have the higher capital-output ratio. (1)

Thus, factory production is characterized as capital-intensive while small-scale production is characterized as labor-intensive. But the solution of the question as to what is preferable under one or another set of concrete conditions, and as to where the boundaries of the maximum effectiveness of using one or the other are, presents considerable difficulty. If we are to approach this question without preconceived notions, the need naturally arises to make some kind of comparison and to select, from among numerous indicators characterizing one or the other mode of production, one or several basic indicators that are most important precisely under the given conditions. In short, it is required to determine the criterion of the effectiveness of capital investments in one or the other type of production.

The selection of a capital investment criterion is the touchstone that is used to test all investigations concerning the prospects for the economic development of economically underdeveloped countries, attempts to plan their economies, and assessments of the role of one or another sector and branch in social reproduction. Although it is very important for any country, in the developing countries, with their narrow capital accumulation base, this question becomes one of the most vital. Naturally, many foreign economists — including bourgeois economists, whose works claim to make a serious approach to the problems of underdeveloped countries — attempt to answer this question. "There is hardly any other question in today's literature on the problems of economic development that evokes so much interest and divergence of opinion as the question of investment criteria," (2) writes Yale University economist Gustav Ranis.

It should be pointed out that the overwhelming majority of students of this problem approach it from a technico-economic point of view. The neglect of the sociopolitical aspects of the problem seen in the works of bourgeois economists will hardly further the correct solution of the problem. As we know, small-scale industrial production and the enormous stratum of the urban petty bourgeoisie connected with it, as well as the prospects for the existence and evolution of this stratum, is not only an economic problem; it is an important social problem as well. The question of the fate of small-scale production in developing countries can only be resolved in close conjunction with the general problems in the socioeconomic development of these countries. The markedly pronounced technicism that is characteristic of most bourgeois works unquestionably lowers their worth.

There is still another approach to this problem, an approach that can be called socioethical. In our opinion, it is utterly unacceptable because its proponents abstract from pressing practical problems, renounce all manner of economic calculation, and in principle oppose machine industry, favoring handicraft production. The adherents of such views are extremely numerous, especially in Asian countries.

"The purely idealistic school," Indian economists Lakdawala and Sandesara write, "favors the regeneration and encouragement of domestic and small-scale industry as a general program for the reorganization of the total socioeconomic structure of society on the 'basis of decentralization,' which more or less corresponds to the ideals of the old 'village commune.' A return to the primitive order with its minimal demands and standard of living can be considered utterly impossible in this rapidly changing world, of which we are a part, and which is moving toward prosperity...." (3) It is clear that the views of the "purely idealistic school" have no scientific or practical value and generally are a component part of various religious-ethical teachings. They are very widespread in the developing countries, however, and must without question be considered in resolving the fate of small-scale commodity production in these countries.

Of course, the most interesting are the attempts to find economic criteria in the assessment of the effectiveness of various technologies. In this connection, we shall discuss certain works by foreign economists.

A. Kahn, Investment Criteria
in Development Programs (4)

Essentially, the serious postwar discussion on the question of using capital-intensive and labor-

intensive production modes begins with this work. It would hardly be advisable to take any earlier works, because that would lead us too far afield. Alfred Kahn himself, by the way, polemicizes with his predecessors, especially with the American economists Buchanan and Pollack.

The author opposes the simplistic approach of these economists to the selection of objects for investments on the basis of the "output-capital" ratio. This approach led Buchanan and Pollack to the conclusion that "nations reconstructing or developing their economies must economize on deficit capital resources and concentrate their attention on investments in objects that are not capital-intensive" (pp. 38-39) — in other words, they must chiefly develop small-scale production with a low level of mechanization.

Kahn also considers incorrect the approach from the point of view of "capital turnover" or the "profit-capital" ratio. "The capital turnover criterion," he writes, "is useless for determining that point at which it is necessary to cease to replace a resource that is in short supply by a resource that is available in abundance" (p. 40). Instead, Alfred Kahn proposes his criterion, which he calls "social marginal productivity" or SMP. By this is meant the "net contribution of a marginal unit (scarce resource) to the national product and not simply that part of the contribution (or of its value) that goes to the private investor" (p. 39). As pointed out by Hollis B. Chenery, a later investigator of this question, Kahn's SMP criterion in practice reduces to determining the sum of increment in national income per unit of capital investment. (5)

Kahn observes that the "social marginal productivity" criterion complicates the question of choosing between capital-intensive and labor-intensive modes of production. "The availability of one or another natural resource, skilled cadres, certain climatic conditions, or the importance of the production of one or another product can lead to an increase in the social marginal productivity of capital in the more capital-intensive production modes as compared with other, less capital-intensive modes. The superiority of one technology over another and the inadequacies of the total substitution of labor for capital may evoke the need for the greater use of capital" (e.g., railroads and rickshaws). Thus, to Kahn's way of thinking, the simple and not always correct criterion of "greater output per unit of capital investment" must be replaced by a more flexible criterion of "social purpose-fulness" (p. 40).

However, when Alfred Kahn proceeds from abstract "social marginal productivity" to a concrete situation, he proves to be very close to Buchanan and Pollack, whom he criticized. In particular, in reviewing the situation in the developing countries, he writes: "In certain regions, labor may actually have a zero evaluation. Clearly this does not refer to all countries.... However, in many of them there is disguised unemployment in agriculture, and one of the conditions in the program for increasing agricultural output is the elimination of this surplus labor force. To the extent that this labor can replace capital...the social marginal productivity of labor will equal zero. Or in another case, if to bring this labor force into action small capital investments are required (e.g., in the organization of the necessary transport, housing, training, or simple work tools), the social marginal productivity will be high for the minimal investments and zero in the case of further capital outlays that economize on labor. Accordingly, beyond a certain critical point, the 'social marginal productivity' principle (SMP) will again coincide with the Buchanan-Pollack rule" (p. 40). In other words, for developing countries beset by a shortage of capital and a "surplus" labor force, the SMP principle prescribes the principal development of production forms with a low level of mechanization.

Alfred Kahn was one of the first to try to coordinate the problem of the criterion of selecting objects for investment with the problem of foreign currency resources. In his treatment, however, this problem is viewed not so much from the position of the economic development of the country itself and the greatest effectiveness of expending deficit foreign currency reserves as from the point of view of the lending

nations: the degree to which the ability to pay of a given nation would increase as a result of one or another application of the loans received by it. "In all cases, the problem is one of maximum utilization of limited resources," he writes. "The ability of the country to pay off foreign loans and interest on them depends (in the long haul) on how imported capital is used in order to achieve a maximum contribution to the national product. Only social marginal productivity and not capital turnover can serve as the evaluation of this" (p. 42).

It should be pointed out that in Kahn's work there is only a general formulation of the question of "social marginal productivity," and any kind of quantitative analysis of the investigated phenomenon is totally lacking.

Hollis B. Chenery, The Application of Investment Criteria (6)

Essentially this work further develops and makes more specific the concept of "social marginal productivity" — SMP (but under the name "marginal social product"), even though the treatment of this criterion does differ in certain ways from that of Kahn.

As his point of departure, Chenery takes the function of well-being:

$$U = U(Y, B, D...),\qquad (1)$$

where U is the indicator of public well-being; Y is the effect of a given capital investment on national income; B is the overall net effect on the balance of payments; and D is the effect on the distribution of income.

Increment U, corresponding to a given increment in capital investments, will equal

$$\Delta U = \frac{\partial U}{\partial Y}\Delta Y + \frac{\partial U}{\partial B}\Delta B + \frac{\partial U}{\partial D}\Delta D + \dots$$

Measuring U in the same units as the national income and dividing the above expression by $\partial U/\partial Y = 1$, we obtain

$$\Delta U = \Delta Y + \frac{\partial Y}{\partial B}\Delta B + \frac{\partial Y}{\partial D}\Delta D + \dots \qquad (2)$$

For the sake of simplicity Chenery subsequently omits all variables except Y and B.

In Formula 2, it is precisely ΔU that denotes the "marginal social product." Unlike Kahn, for whom the expression SMP is equivalent to the expression ΔY, or to the increment in national income, Chenery considers it necessary to include the effect of capital investments on the balance of payments in the SMP concept:

$$SMP = \Delta U = \Delta Y + r\Delta B. \qquad (3)$$

Parameter r denotes the coefficient of substitutability between Y and B, or the premium for foreign currency proceeds as compared with the same value expressed in national currency. A change in valuation r can influence the state of the balance of payments. Thus, in order to offset the balance of payments for one or another period, the premium for foreign currency can be raised, etc.

Chenery gives a more detailed expression for SMP, which is an expanded expression of Formula 3:

$$SMP = \frac{X+E-M_I}{K} - \frac{L+M_D+O}{K} + \frac{r}{K}(aB_1 + B_2) \\ = \frac{V}{K} - \frac{C}{K} + \frac{rB}{K}, \qquad (4)$$

where SMP is the annual increment in national income (plus the increment in foreign currency proceeds) from the marginal unit of capital investments in a given production mode; K is the increment in capital investments; X is the increment in the internal market value of the output; E is the additional value of the exported part of the output, conditioned by differences in the purchasing power of currencies; M_I is the value of imported materials; L is outlays for wages; M_D is the value of own materials; O is other costs, including depreciation of capital; V is the increment of value created within the country = $X + E - M_I$; C is the overall value of own factors of production = $L + M_D + O$; B is the overall effect on the balance of payments = $aB_1 + B_2$; B_1 is the primary ("incremental") effect of capital investments on the balance of

payments; B_2 is the effect of the subsequent exploitation of capital investments ("operational") on the balance of payments; and a is the repayment of loans and interest on them.

Formula 4 can be rewritten in the following form:

$$SMP = \left(\frac{V}{K}\right) \cdot \left(\frac{V-C}{V}\right) + \left(\frac{rB}{K}\right), \qquad (5)$$

where V/K is the "output-capital" ratio; $\frac{V-C}{V}$ is the coefficient of the degree to which the value of the product exceeds the costs; and rB/K is the foreign trade effect per unit of capital investments.

Using Formulas 4 and 5, Chenery evaluates various projects in Greece and Italy (7) and in so doing applies this principle to the evaluation of projects relating not only to a single branch but also to various branches.

It is not difficult to see that, in the final analysis, Chenery's "marginal social product" criterion may be reduced to an increase in national income per unit of capital investment. A peculiarity of his interpretation of the given criterion is the greater emphasis of that part of the product obtained as a result of capital investments that can be realized in foreign currency and, correspondingly, greater attention to the outlays of foreign currency that one or another project requires. Function U may be expanded on the basis of additional factors (B, D...), but nonetheless the basic factor in it continues to be the increment in the national income. Chenery himself notes that his criterion makes the most sense when it is a matter of choosing between projects relating to different branches. But as regards the selection of projects differing in the degree of capital-intensiveness within a single branch, in his opinion this criterion can be reduced to the selection of the maximum income per unit of capital investment or even the maximum "output-capital" ratio, because all other factors, including the foreign trade effect on the balance of payments, change but slightly in the given case and can be neglected. In other words, in Chenery's opinion, if it is necessary to choose from among various projects within a single branch, one may use both Kahn's criterion (national income) as well as the criterion of Buchanan-Pollack ("output-capital"). Chenery even argues this point with Kahn: "In his criticism of the conclusions of Buchanan and Pollack, Kahn points out that 'social marginal productivity' of capital is not correlated with the 'output-capital' ratio." "This statement is correct," Chenery writes, "when it is a matter of all branches as a whole. However, this does not preclude the use of the latter ratio in selected cases. The 'output-capital' ratio is useful, in particular, for choosing between projects belonging to the same branch." "Economy in the use of capital," the author notes, "may in the given case be the decisive consideration" (p. 87).

In addition to the SMP criterion in its general form, as presented by Formulas 4 and 5, or in concretized form by "national income-capital" or "output-capital" ratios, Chenery observes that it is also necessary to consider the "social value" of investments (p. 93). This includes first the necessity of using surplus resources (manpower, certain natural resources, etc.) and of economizing on limited resources (fixed capital, electric power, transport, industrial materials in short supply). It should be noted, however, that nowhere does Chenery make employment an objective function. In his treatment of it, an increase in employment looks like a by-product of that selection of investment that is dictated by the SMP criterion.

In a later work, written in conjunction with P. Clark, Chenery turns once more to the question of investment criteria, simplifying the "social marginal product" to the national product that can be obtained from one or another type of productive activity. Scarce resources, as well as the goals that it is desirable to attain at the same time (e.g., increased employment), are viewed as constraints on the objective function. "In planning economic development, the function being maximized almost always represents the national product. Other factors referred to above (employment, the balance of payments, income distribution, etc.) can be viewed as constraints that determine the solution of the basic

problem. Other constraints are the desired structure of commodity consumption, the availability of manpower and natural resources, the supply of capital (namely, savings within the country plus foreign loans)." (8)

Returning to the first work of Chenery that we examined, we should note his detailed elaboration of the problem of quantitative measurement of the "general effect of capital investments on the balance of payments." Here, however, we shall not examine this question because it introduces nothing new to what was said above concerning the principles in Chenery's approach to the problem of selecting objects for capital investment in the developing countries.

W. Galenson and H. Leibenstein, Investment Criteria, Productivity and Economic Development (9)

This work presents serious argumentation in defense of the development of exclusively modern forms of production, including the economically underdeveloped countries. The authors criticize the approach to the investment plan both from the point of view of the maximization of output and from the point of view of the maximization of employment. The principle of "social marginal productivity" advanced as a criterion of capital investment in the works of Alfred Kahn, Hollis B. Chenery, and others is subjected to critical analysis.

As Galenson and Leibenstein point out, the SMP principle presupposes three basic requirements:

(1) maximum initial "output-capital" ratio;

(2) maximum "labor-capital" ratio, or the maximization of employment per unit of capital investment;

(3) maximum "output of export goods-capital investment" ratio (p. 346).

The work examines the first two requirements, because the third is connected not only with the nature of the distribution of capital outlays but also with a number of other internal and external factors.

The authors note that the selection from among a number of branches and technological modes of those that are distinguished by the highest initial output per unit of capital investment can lead to an incorrect general result because no consideration is given to another characteristic of branches and technological modes — different rates of growth of accumulation and, correspondingly, of return on capital investments in the process of their extended use. A branch or technological mode of production, rejected during the initial period for their low return or low "output-capital" coefficient, can, over a certain period, turn out a greater volume of output than selected branches with high initial output. This is why Galenson and Leibenstein emphasize that "in determining social marginal productivity, we must consider the effect of new capital investments on the output indicator for an undetermined future period of time and not only for the initial period" (p. 346).

The authors point out that the second SMP requirement can be similarly reviewed. In development, a branch of industry or a technological production mode that at present guarantees the maximum employment may prove to be by no means optimal among the possible variants. As a basis of differences between static and dynamic indicators of effectiveness (output in one case, employment in the other) of one or another branch or technological mode, there is assumed, first of all, their varying capacity for accumulation, or varying share of accumulation in the product they create. And these circumstances are precisely the ones that are not considered in the basic SMP requirements.

The authors point out that the application of the SMP principle leads to the "perpetuation of low labor productivity." Yet "it is precisely high labor productivity that makes possible a high standard of living" (p. 351).

In the opinion of Galenson and Leibenstein, the criteria of capital investment effectiveness, based on the above-enumerated SMP requirements, suffer from the following shortcomings: (1) they stress capital and not labor, the productive force of capital and not labor productivity; (2) these criteria accentuate initial output

and not the accumulation norm that determines the size of capital investment and the dimensions of output in the future — in other words, for the observance of the formal SMP requirements, the composition of final product is a matter of indifference, while it is precisely this factor that determines the norm of accumulation; and (3) the criteria do not consider changes in factors other than capital.

As a criterion eliminating these shortcomings the authors propose their own "marginal per capita reinvestment quotient," the essence of which reduces to the selection of such a method of distributing capital investments as would guarantee maximum labor productivity per worker at the end of a given period. Galenson and Leibenstein point out that this requires the maximization of the amount of capital per worker and the level of skill, knowledge, energy, and "adaptability" of the worker (p. 351). In this connection it is necessary that the rates of capital accumulation overtake the rate at which the labor force grows in number.

Like most of their bourgeois colleagues, Galenson and Leibenstein consider population growth in presently underdeveloped countries a serious obstacle to economic development. This obstacle supposedly lies in the fact that the growth of the population and the increase in its employment in the production process reduce the amount of capital per worker. In the estimation of the authors, the proper application of capital can also help here. The point is that in proportion to the growth of the consumption level, in the economically underdeveloped countries the mortality rate declines at a relatively greater pace than the birthrate increases, and as a result the overall population growth rate is accelerated. "Therefore, the greater the gap between production and consumption, the slower the rate of population growth and the less is the dilution of capital" (p. 352).

In the opinion of Galenson and Leibenstein, the relative reduction of population growth is also served by such a distribution of capital investments as would promote urbanization since, as a rule, the latter entails a reduction in the rate of the population growth owing to the small size of the families of urban residents, etc.

The crux of these arguments is again only a defense of the development of modern forms of industrial production and against backward, lower forms of entrepreneurial activities, including village crafts. Not contenting themselves with purely economic reasons, however, the authors also employ neo-Malthusian argumentation.

Developing their views further, Galenson and Leibenstein maintain that as the wage level increases, the use of highly productive equipment becomes more advantageous both in terms of output and employment.

To reflect this, the following formula is presented:

$$\varepsilon_{t+1} = \varepsilon_1 \left(1 + \frac{P - ew}{c}\right)^t,$$

where ε_{t+1} is employment in year $t + 1$; ε_1 is employment in the initial (base) year; P is net output per machine; e is the number of workers per machine; w is the wage rate; c is the cost of the machine.

In itself, this formula expresses nothing else but the generally known truth: the greater the part of the output of a branch of industry or society that goes into reinvestment, the more rapid will be the process of capital accumulation and, accordingly, employment growth (p. 358). The value of this formula lies in the fact that it graphically illustrates one of the well-known economic principles, specifically, "the higher the wage level, the more advantage there is to applying capital-intensive equipment with respect to employment" (p. 359). By substituting corresponding figures in the above formula, this conclusion can be verified.

Further, the authors criticize the SMP principle for in fact ignoring differences in the methods of industrial development in determining the effectiveness of capital investment. "It is far from being a matter of indifference," they write, "whether capital investments are distributed, let us say, for the production of pig iron and steel or for the production of textiles. In their

recommendations, the IBRD missions are too prone to believe that the investment of funds in the development of branches of the light industry, e.g., those that use local raw materials, in the final analysis will in some inexplicable way lead to economic development" (p. 361).

The logic of the cited arguments of Galenson and Leibenstein is evident. It is unquestionable, however, that they can only be viewed as a general approach to the problems of developing countries. In our estimation, it would be incorrect to see in them methodological instructions for all actual cases. Incidentally, the authors themselves take note of this: "Strictly speaking, neither the application of a SMP criterion in its orthodox interpretation nor the application of our own criteria will automatically lead to the creation of a production model that would maximize industrial development" (p. 361). And elsewhere: "...criteria expressed by the marginal per capita reinvestment quotient and the principle concerning the high 'capital-labor' ratio are suitable general indicators for compiling programs of economic development" (p. 367).

The vulnerability of such a general approach is felt immediately as we descend from the theoretical heights to the vital everyday concerns of the developing countries. Galenson and Leibenstein themselves note a number of special conditions existing in the economically underdeveloped countries — conditions that hinder the unconditional utilization of their criteria for investment distribution. Among these special conditions, Galenson and Leibenstein name the surplus of manpower and its corresponding cheapness in the economically underdeveloped countries. As we know, this circumstance does not stimulate the use of costly, albeit more productive, equipment and better paid labor.

"In such situations," the authors write, "the employment of as large a number of workers as possible is not only economically justified but is also desirable from the social point of view" (p. 368).

Another condition — the lack of a skilled labor force — is also a hindrance to the growth of labor productivity. True, the authors note that difficulties in this respect are exaggerated and that the Soviet experience attests to the possibility of a relatively rapid elimination of this shortage. Nonetheless it does exist at the present time and must be reckoned with. A shortage of skilled cadres is particularly felt in large-scale modern industry, whereas the lowest forms of industrial production are better supplied with cadres owing to the long existence of these forms.

Unquestionably, in the process of the economic development of these countries, the conditions in them will increasingly approach those under which it will be possible to follow directly the criterion of maximum labor productivity. In particular, the struggle of the working class to raise living standards will lead to an increase in the overall amount of wages and will thus create a stimulus for the use of modern, highly productive equipment. This will also be furthered by rather intensive industrial development leading, first, to an ever greater absorption of the surplus labor force and, second, to the urbanization of an ever increasing part of the population. At the present time, however, the problem of employment and capital investment cannot be considered to be solved solely on the basis of principles and criteria proposed by Galenson and Leibenstein.

A. K. Sen, Choice of Techniques. An Aspect of the Theory of Planned Economic Development (10)

In our estimation, this work is the most solid piece of research in this area. We shall subsequently turn to Sen's concrete elaborations. Here we shall analyze only general principles recommended by the author for selecting the mode of production.

As Sen notes, the investment policy of the government in an economically underdeveloped country incorporates three basic aspects: (1) the determination of the size of the national income allocated for extended reproduction; (2) the distribution of capital investments among various branches of the national economy; and (3) the selection of techniques that must embody the

allocated capital investments. All three aspects are closely interrelated. In particular, "the dimensions of the capital investments that we will be able to make in the future depend directly on our selection from among various modes of production that differ in the degree of capital-intensiveness and the resulting differences in the formation of a 'surplus'" (p. 20). In this connection, Sen emphasizes the importance of elaborating the problem of the selection of the technological mode as one of the basic problems of economic policy.

Unlike the foreign economists referred to above, Sen does not consider it possible to give any kind of a single definite answer to the question as to what is preferable for the economically underdeveloped nation: small-scale production promoting an increase in employment and very frequently in the gross product, or modern forms of production maximizing the surplus product and, accordingly, the economic growth rates. In Sen's opinion, in the economically underdeveloped country only the concrete conditions and requirements of the economy can determine this selection. Sen therefore examines two basic possibilities: (1) the need to maximize output, and (2) the need to maximize the dimensions of the "surplus," or of the surplus product.

In order to avoid errors linked to prices and price formation, Sen proceeds from the following assumptions. Capital-intensiveness (or capital available per worker) constitutes the number of work hours necessary to supply one worker with the means of production in the sector producing the final product. It is assumed that a single final product — grain — is being produced. Wages, the newly created product, and profit are reflected in this final product. Further, it is established that one and the same product is produced by two technological modes: L and H. The second mode is more capital-intensive than the first. The following basic conditions are introduced to verify the effectiveness of both methods.

Mode L will yield a larger, equal, or lesser initial volume of output than mode H if

$$\frac{P_c}{a} >, = \text{ or } < \frac{P'_c}{a'}, \text{ i.e.,}$$

$$\frac{P_c}{P'_c} >, = \text{ or } < \frac{a}{a'}. \quad \text{(Condition I)}$$

Sen notes: "From this it does not follow, however, that the mode that initially yields the greater output will yield a greater volume of output in succeeding periods as well" (p. 23). For this it is also necessary to know what kind of "surplus" for expanding production can be obtained by this mode.

Mode L will yield a larger, equal, or lesser increment in the "surplus" than mode H if

$$\frac{P_c - w}{a} >, = \text{ or } < \frac{P'_c - w}{a'}, \text{ i.e.,}$$

$$\frac{P_c - w}{P'_c - w} >, = \text{ or } < \frac{a}{a'}; \quad \text{(Condition II)}$$

where P_c is output per worker during a given period; a is capital available per worker in the sector producing the final product (grain); and w is real wages per worker during a given period.

For mode H, the same designations are used with a prime. For the sake of simplicity, in all cases the net rather than the gross product is taken. Thus, product = wages + surplus product, or

$$P_c = w + N.$$

What is the economic meaning of the first and second conditions? If we are interested in immediately increasing consumption, Sen says, it is necessary to maximize the "net output–capital" ratio (Condition I). If we are interested in development in the future and if we have unlimited time at our disposal, it is necessary to maximize the size of "the surplus" (or growth rate), because in this case, provided sufficient activity exists for a period, the overall sum of the produced output will be greater than in the case where we maximize the size of the product (Condition II). The solution of the problem is made easier, Sen notes, if the time factor is introduced in our reasoning, delimiting that interval

within which we wish to maximize overall output (p. 31).

We shall examine the simplest model proposed by Sen and, for the sake of brevity, lay aside the purely demonstrative aspect of the problem and assumptions made by the author. The model has the following form:

$$Y_1 = \bar{S} \cdot f$$
$$S_1 = \bar{S}(f - x)$$
$$Y_2 = Y_1 + S_1 \cdot f = \bar{S} \cdot f \cdot (1 + f - x)$$
$$S_2 = \bar{S}(f - x)(1 + f - x)$$
$$\cdots \cdots \cdots \cdots$$
$$Y_n = \bar{S} \cdot f \cdot (1 + f - x)^{n-1}$$
$$S_n = \bar{S} \cdot (f - x)(1 + f - x)^{n-1}$$
$$A_n = \sum_{p=1}^{n} Y_p = \bar{S} \cdot f \cdot [1 + (1 + f - x) +$$
$$+ (1 + f - x)^2 + \ldots + (1 + f - x)^{n-1}] = \bar{S} \cdot f \frac{(1 + f - x)^n - 1}{f - x},$$

where x is the amount of labor used in the production of grain with the aid of one machine; $f(x)$ is annual output with the aid of one machine (in the formula abbreviated to f); Y_p is overall output during year p (p = 1, 2 ... n); A_n is aggregate output for n years; $\bar{S}$ is the initial "surplus" of grain (= initial volume of capital investments) — subsequently, the branch develops solely on the basis of its own accumulation; and S_p is the overall "surplus" of grain in year p.

The essence of the problem lies in the selection of optimal capital-intensiveness $1/x$. In this process, three criteria may be used: A — maximization of initial output (Y_1); B — maximization of growth rates (G); and C — maximization of aggregate output during n years A_n (p. 35).

Criterion A:

$$Y_1 = \bar{S} \cdot f.$$

Y_1 is maximized when $dY_1/dx = 0$ and also $d^2Y_1/dx^2 < 0$, by selecting x satisfying the conditions:

$$f'(x) = 0, \quad f''(x) < 0.$$

Criterion B:

$$G = \frac{Y_n - Y_{n-1}}{Y_{n-1}} = \frac{S_{n-1} \cdot f}{Y_{n-1}} = f - x.$$

G is maximized by finding such x with which $f'(x) = 1$ and also $f''(x) < 0$.

Criterion C:

$$A_n = \overline{S} \cdot f \frac{(1+f-x)^n - 1}{f - x}.$$

A_n is maximized when $dA_n/dx = 0$ and also $d^2A_n/dx^2 < 0$.

It is necessary to find x such that

$$\frac{dA_n}{dx} = \overline{S} \cdot f' \frac{(1+f-x)^n - 1}{f-x} + \overline{S} \cdot f$$

$$\times \frac{(f-x)(f'-1)n(1+f-x)^{n-1} - (f'-1)[(1+f-x)^n - 1]}{(f-x)^2} = 0,$$

or

$$(1+f-x)^{n-1} \cdot [n \cdot f(f-x) \cdot (f'-1) + (1+f-x)(f-f' \cdot x)] - (f-f' \cdot x) = 0.$$

Sen observes that criteria A and B may be viewed as particular cases of criterion C. If the number of years n = 1, then the condition of maximality of criterion C is reduced to $f'(x) = 0$, which corresponds to criterion A. On the other hand, if n is very great, the condition of maximality reduces to $f'(x) = 1$, which corresponds to criterion B (p. 36).

Other of Sen's models represent the development and complication of the given simplest model by various additional conditions. Thus, in the intersector model, capital-intensiveness is selected for several sectors and not merely for one. Let us say that there are three branches: branch C producing grain (or some other consumer good); branch I producing machines for C; and branch J producing machines for I. In this case, relationships are plotted linking capital-intensiveness in I (a) with capital intensiveness in J (b). The production function for branch I is:

$$a = f(b).$$

Aggregate output A is maximized in branch C for the period of time n, and the problem reduces to that of finding such b as will maximize A.

Provided that the production function is continuous, A reaches a maximum with the observance of requirement

$$\frac{\partial A}{\partial b} = 0,$$

and also

$$\frac{\partial^2 A}{\partial b^2} < 0.$$

If the function is discrete, extremality criterion $\partial A/\partial b = 0$ is inapplicable. In this case, we search a number of alternative values of b and choose the one that maximizes aggregate output (p. 41).

When the model becomes more complicated (several raw materials, use of other resources in addition to labor and capital, etc.), it is more convenient to represent it in matrix form. With the given capital investments of a given year, the increment in output during the following year will be:

$$(X_1) = [c]^{-1}(\overline{S}_0).$$

Accordingly, the "surplus" or surplus product created with the help of the given capital investments is:

$$(S_1) = (X_1) - [b] \cdot (X_1) = [1 - b] \cdot [c]^{-1}(\overline{S}_0),$$

where $(\overline{S}_0)$ is the aggregate of the goods and services (including intermediate products) that can be used for capital investments in a given year; [c] is the matrix of fixed capital expenditure coefficients ("capital-output" coefficients); and [b] is the matrix of current expenditure coefficients (including labor).

The problem of maximizing output or "surplus" now lies in the selection of the optimal combination [1 − b] and [c], which, in fact, is analogous to the selection of the optimal relationship $(P_c - w)$, or capital-intensiveness a and b in the simplest forms of the model examined above.

In Sen's opinion, a very important factor influencing the selection of capital investments in capital-intensive or labor-intensive techniques is the dependence of each existing mode of production on the amounts of that equipment and those materials that must be imported. Sen notes: "'Mechanized' industry, as a rule, requires very high outlays in foreign currency, while small-scale (manual weaving, primitive oil extraction facilities) can almost entirely get along with instruments and tools of labor produced within the country." "In this case, foreign currency considerations may be dominant until such time as the country develops its own production of the means of production" (p. 71).

While making a general assessment of Sen's approach to the problem, two circumstances should be noted. Of all works we have investigated, Sen's study unquestionably presents the most developed apparatus for determining the maximum effectiveness of capital investments, depending on the selection of techniques. Sen's work, however, is based on an already given criterion for such selection. In one case this may be the maximization of the initial output, in another — maximization of the "surplus," or surplus product, for the attainment of highest growth rates in a branch, while in a third — maximization of the global product for a number of years. Evidently Sen himself regards the latter criterion to be the most important and gives it the greatest amount of attention. The latter criterion, however, presupposes that, depending on the duration of the given period of time, technological production modes that are completely different in terms of their economic results can be selected. If the time period is small, technology will be selected that will yield the greatest initial output but that will be far from optimal with respect to the yield in surplus product, i.e., technology answering criterion A. On the other hand, if the selected period is infinitely great, it is a matter of selecting technology corresponding to criterion B. Clearly the selection between criteria B and C becomes much easier if the aim of the given investments is determined in time. In this case, however, an additional problem arises: the development of criteria and valuations for the selection of the time period

itself, during which it is proposed to make the most effective use of the capital investments.

Thus, even the most complete, and, in our estimation, the most interesting of all existing foreign works devoted to the problem that is of concern to us, does not answer the question as to just what should serve as a guide in the selection of one or another technological mode, i.e., the question as to the sum of those economic conditions that can serve as a yardstick of the effectiveness and advisability of the plan we have adopted for capital investments within a single branch.

R. Balakrishna, Review of Economic Growth in India (11)

The author observes that India's economy is characterized by "dualism" — by the existence of "organized" capitalist and "unorganized" small-scale commodity sectors. In the opinion of R. Balakrishna, "there is no harm whatsoever in the existence of a dual economy as long as the gap between the two sectors is not great. One sector may stimulate another if they are within reach of one another" (p. 158). At the same time he notes that the average consumer must bear the burden of the financial support of the "unorganized" sector that is not in a position to compete.

Professor Balakrishna's credo concerning the place of the "unorganized" sector in the economy of an underdeveloped country reduces to three basic points: (1) the need to develop modern heavy industry that not only will serve as the basis for all future development but will also promote conditions favorable to the "unorganized" sector; (2) the entire economy, however, should not be built solely on the modern technology of the factory industry; (3) in the production of consumer goods, primary emphasis should be placed on small-scale industry. For the rational development of the latter, it is necessary to improve its existing technology (p. 162).

Balakrishna is not entirely clear on the question as to the selection of capital investment

62

criteria (the "capital-intensive versus labor-intensive production" dilemma). "The choice between the modern technology of factory production and obsolescent technology in small-scale and handicraft production also depends on the goals that those planning the development set themselves. They may be confronted with the goal of providing either employment or development.... Unquestionably employment can be a result of development, but between one and the other a time lag will be inevitable if the structure of capital investments is oriented toward capital-intensive processes. Development may or may not take place if the structure of capital investment is oriented toward employment. With this in mind, the goal of government policy must be clearly defined without mixing various tasks. If unemployment is truly a brake on development, the policy for the transitional period should particularly place greater emphasis on employment. Everything must be done, however, so that in the final analysis the transitional policy as well would further development" (p. 160).

Despite the fact that Balakrishna admits the possibility of planning capital investments for securing greater employment as a main goal, he warns against enthusiasm for forms of production with a low level of mechanization. On the surface, these forms would seem to be enticing — with negligible capital investments they provide employment for a large number of workers. Upon closer examination, however, they prove to be utterly ineffective and are justified neither from the point of view of even those small capital investments that they need, from the point of view of organizational efforts, nor the more so from the point of view of the colossal expenditure of human resources. "Any manner of sentimental approach to obsolescent forms of production is incompatible with progress," the author writes. "Capital investments in these forms are not rational and not only are they useless, they are also harmful to the development of the economy. The immense amount of attention devoted, e.g., to the 'Ambar Charkha experiment' (handloom) is evidence of a striving to observe the form of this path of development rather than its goals" (pp. 169-170).

R. Balakrishna emphasizes the temporary nature of the use of certain forms of production, particularly in small-scale production. "Any path of development that may be approved at the beginning of the planning period," he indicates, "is not necessarily a most suitable one in the latter stages of development. Economic development itself will propose a new path because the factors that determine it change in their relative significance. With the growth in labor productivity, capital accumulation may become easier, and with a growth in income and a rise in the standard of living, labor may become more expensive. In this stage, it will not be cheaper to use labor-intensive production methods. On the other hand, it will not be so difficult to introduce capital-intensive production methods, and the entire economy will gravitate toward maximal technological effectiveness. Therefore, the path of development that is most acceptable at the beginning of the growth period can be only a temporary measure" (p. 170).

D. Lakdawala and J. Sandesara, Small Industry in a Big City (12)

On the whole, the authors of this work support production with a low level of mechanization. Their argumentation in favor of small-scale industry, which, by the way, is widely circulated in India and other developing countries, (13) can be reduced to the following.

First: the great potential for employment that small-scale industry promises (p. 5). The possibility of employing a considerable number of workers on existing meager capital — this is the main argument resorted to by all active proponents of small-scale production, and by those official circles in developing countries which support the preservation and development of labor-intensive forms of production.

Second: small-scale industry, scattered over a large area, sometimes far from large industrial centers, can provide for the needs of small local markets better than the factory industry. In the opinion of Lakdawala and Sandesara, this will lead to a great economy in outlays of a social and economic nature (p. 7).

Third: the use of internally produced implements and means of labor by small-scale industry makes it possible to economize part of the foreign currency that is in short supply.

Lakdawala and Sandesara refute the argument directed against small-scale production to the effect that "the reinvested surplus per worker in labor-intensive small-scale industry will be relatively less and that, in general, small-scale industry ... is associated with a low capacity for surplus formation." "In answer to this," the authors write, "it may be pointed out that even though the surplus per worker will be greater when modern technology is used, the overall surplus produced in the economy (national economy) through a network of enterprises with labor-intensive technology may be still higher. (14) The government, as the organizer of economic progress, can mobilize this fund with the aid of a suitable apparatus and direct it to the desired spheres" (p. 6).

Baljit Singh, The Economics of Small-Scale Industries (15)

B. Singh, a member of the Program Study Committee of the Indian planning commission, is the author of a number of books on problems of Indian economics. This book represents a summary statistical study of small-scale industry in one of the most important centers of this industry — Moradabad.

Singh notes that in the developing countries there is strong argument in favor of small-scale industry, based on the fact that because "the equipment used by this industry is less capital-intensive, this industry is more suitable to countries with a shortage of capital" (p. 1). Singh does not agree, however, with this formulation of the question. The very "conception of capital-intensiveness," he notes, is used in two aspects: (1) as the amount of capital per worker or the "capital-labor" ratio (in our terminology, capital-intensiveness) and (2) as the amount of capital per unit of output, i.e., "capital-output ratio." Singh writes that these two aspects need not

necessarily coincide. Small-scale industry can occupy an adequate place only if it proves to be less capital-intensive in both senses.

"The economic criterion for the selection of the technological mode in the process of planning can be nothing other than minimal capital per unit of output," writes Singh. "If there is a contradiction (between the two aspects of this ratio — S. K.), the selection must clearly be in favor of technology requiring smaller capital outlays per unit of output rather than in favor of technology with lower capital outlays per worker" (p. 2). From this also follows the basic requirement that Singh makes of small-scale industry: "If small-scale and handicraft industry is given some kind of role in the planned development of underdeveloped countries, its technology must satisfy the criterion for lower capital per unit of output. The ignoring of this criterion very frequently leads to results that do not withstand criticism. By way of an example, the second five-year plan of our own country can be cited. The role assigned to small-scale industry in the plan and the preference given the 'Ambar Charkha' (handloom) over modern textile equipment are fruitless and in the future will entail higher outlays, both socially and economically."

Singh believes that the technology of small-scale industry can find great application in the production of consumer goods, where it promises a relatively low amount of capital both per worker and per unit of output. But as regards the production of the means of production, owing to various technical restrictions, "the selection of technology in it can rarely be based exclusively on the economic criterion of a minimal capital-output ratio" (p. 3).

John Fei and Gustav Ranis, Innovation, Capital Accumulation and Economic Development (16)

Yale University economists J. Fei and Gustav Ranis substantiate the necessity for using labor-intensive production processes in the early stages of development of the underdeveloped economy. Their reasoning is as follows.

64

For the underdeveloped economy, with its surplus population, high population growth rate, and acute shortage of capital, it is presupposed that the level of real wages will remain unchanged throughout the entire period of formation (a special explanation will be given for this point below). Then the employment growth rate (in industry) may be characterized by the equation

$$\eta_l = \eta_k + \frac{B_L + J}{\varepsilon_{le}}, \qquad (1)$$

where J is the intensiveness of innovation (relative increase in output with capital outlays remaining constant); B_L is the degree of labor-intensiveness or the increase in employment during innovation; J and B_L are assumed to be variable with constant K (capital outlays); ε_{le} is the coefficient of the elasticity of demand for labor; $\eta_l \left(\equiv \frac{dL}{dt} \middle/ L \right)$ is the employment growth rate; and $\eta_k \left(\equiv \frac{dK}{dt} \middle/ K \right)$ is the rate of growth of productive capital or capital accumulation.

Thus employment growth rates in industry depend directly on: (1) capital accumulation, (2) intensiveness of innovation J, and (3) the degree of labor-intensiveness B_L, they are inversely dependent on the coefficient of the elasticity of demand for labor ε_{le}.

It can be noted that the right side of Formula 1 in turn breaks down into two parts. The first is η_k, or the growth in employment in connection with capital accumulation (capital investments). The authors call this part the "radial effect" η_r because on the graph employment growth in connection with growth in capital investments has the form of a line both of whose coordinates increase — both along the abscissa (employment) as well as along the ordinate (capital-output ratio), i.e., it has the form of a line going radially from the center of the coordinates. The second part is $\frac{B_L + J}{\varepsilon_{le}}$, or the growth in employment in connection with the reorganization (innovation) of production, which is not connected with an increase in capital investment. The authors call this part the "horizontal effect" η_h because on

the graph the change in the values of expressions $\frac{B_L + J}{\varepsilon_{le}}$ makes a horizontal line that is parallel to the horizontal axis (employment), with a constant value on the vertical axis (capital). Such a breakdown of the right side of Formula 1 is of great importance in the authors' conclusions. Taken together, the radial and horizontal effects produce a broken line of growth $P_1 P_2 P_3 P_4 \dots$ (see Fig. 1) on the graph.

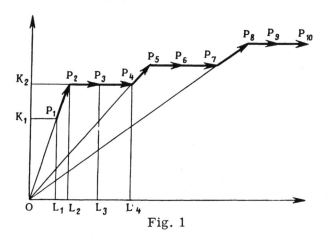

Fig. 1

From Formula 1, the following basic equation is adduced. The authors impart to this equation the force of economic law:

$$g < \eta_l = \eta_k + \frac{B_L + J}{\varepsilon_{le}}. \qquad (2)$$

The authors call this relationship the "critical minimum effort criterion," or CMEC, in the sense that "the nation's efforts reflected in the magnitude of the four factors on the right-hand side must exceed the population growth" (p. 289).

The authors maintain that the nation may not follow this law for some brief period, but that efforts toward economic development cannot be successful if this law is constantly violated over an extended period. By η_l is meant specifically the employment growth rate in industry. Violation of the law means the more rapid growth of the agricultural population, and this, in terms of its meaning, is "contrary to industrialization." It is maintained that CMEC is amenable to influence and control by the government even though the factors in it are amenable to such influence in different degrees. The government can either regulate factors on the right-hand side of the inequality or by "programs for regulating family size" attempt to decrease the population growth g, i.e., the left-hand side of the inequality.

Finally, one more concept discussed by the authors — the "capital-labor" ratio or q = K/L. The growth rate of this ratio is expressed by

$$\eta_q \equiv \frac{dq}{dt} \Big/ q \, .$$

From this definition and Formula 1 it follows that

$$\eta_q = -\frac{B_L + J}{\varepsilon_{le}} \, . \tag{3}$$

Accordingly,

$$\eta_q < 0 \text{ with } B_L + J > 0 \text{ or } B_L > -J.$$
$$\eta_q > 0 \text{ with } B_L + J < 0 \text{ or } B_L < -J.$$

This means that if innovation does not economize on labor to a great extent, then the increment in capital-intensiveness is negative, i.e., there is a lowering of the "capital-labor" ratio (capital-shallowing). On the other hand, if the innovation economizes on labor to a large extent, then there is a positive increment in capital-intensiveness (capital-deepening).

In terms of its meaning, the "capital-labor" ratio growth rate is equal to the value of "horizontal effect," taken with the reversed sign, i.e.,

$$\eta_h = \frac{B_L + J}{\varepsilon_{le}}, \text{ a } \eta_q = -\frac{B_L + J}{\varepsilon_{le}} \, .$$

The authors confirm their theoretical conclusions and their basic thesis on the nature of the growth of employment and capital investment, i.e., on the possibilities of intensive and extensive development, by comparing the statistical materials on Japan and India.

In examining the dynamics of general population growth and of the self-employed [samodeiatel'noe] population working in industry and agriculture in Japan during the period 1888-1930, the authors note that on the basis of this example the CMEC principle is entirely justified: during

the entire period between the second half of the 19th century and the beginning of the 20th century, the rate of growth of the number employed in industry far exceeded the population growth rate. The growth of the population employed in agriculture lagged both behind the general population growth rate and behind the growth rate of those employed in industry. The implementation of the CMEC principle over an extended period of time — the flow of the agricultural population to industry — led to the transformation of Japan into an industrial country.

On the other hand, the authors note, in India the CMEC principle was not implemented during the period 1949-1960, and the population growth rate (with the exception of one year) exceeded the rate of growth of those employed in industry. In connection with this, India cannot "escape the trap of Malthusian law" (p. 294).

But what is the reason? In reply, Fei and Ranis analyze the effect of the overall growth of employment in industry, breaking it down into "radial and horizontal effects"; i.e., they elucidate the factors that have played a basic role in increasing employment.

In illustrating this, the authors compared the development of the economy of Japan in the early stage and that of India. The authors divide the economic history of Japan from 1888 to 1930 into two periods. During the first period — from 1888 to World War I inclusive — the growth of those employed in industry was chiefly a result of the "horizontal effect," i.e., a result of the utilization of labor-intensive production modes. An especially great part of this growth (up to 80%) was accounted for by the "horizontal effect" during the first years of the period. During this period there was a parallel decline in the "capital-labor" coefficient by an amount that, even though not completely coinciding, nonetheless was very close to the value of the "horizontal effect."

During the second period — from the beginning of World War I to 1930 — a reverse phenomenon is observed: a considerable part of the growth of employment that had taken place in industry was now accounted for by the "radial effect," i.e., was explained by new capital in-

66

vestments. In other words, there was an intensification of production. The increase in employment as a result of the selection of labor-
intensive processes in fact not only ceases, but,
on the contrary, the processes with a higher
capital-output ratio attract part of the labor
force from the labor-intensive production units.
Parallel with the negative "horizontal effect"
(η^h) there is an increase in the "capital-labor"
ratio (η_q) or in the amount of capital per worker.

Another situation, though for a shorter historical period, was observed in India. With the
exception of one year (1950), the growth of employment in industry was exclusively a result of
new capital investments or "radial effect." A
continuous increase in the "capital-labor" ratio
was also observed. Thus, Fei and Ranis note,
India chose a path of industrial innovation leading to the economizing of labor, to the curtailment of labor-intensive processes. On the basis
of the Japanese example, which, during the investigated period, attained a high degree of
technical and economic progress, the authors
establish the following general pattern: throughout a certain historical period, the country having a surplus of manpower and a shortage of
capital essentially has to use labor-intensive or,
"in the extreme case, production processes that
do not economize on labor to any great extent"
(extensive development of the economy). At the
end of this period, owing to the absorption of
the "surplus" population by industry, labor is in
short supply, and then there begins another
direction in the development of the economy —
the intensive development of the economy, the
use of more capital-intensive processes, and
the increase in the organic composition of capital.

In the opinion of Fei and Ranis, India violates
this pattern because "from the very beginning of
its efforts in the direction of economic development, it has very clearly resorted to innovation
that greatly economizes on labor, thus creating
a more capital-intensive structure of industry
and ignoring the possibilities for the maximum
utilization of the colossal and rapidly multiply-
ing surplus labor force in agriculture" (p. 297).
The authors aver that the use of the CMEC prin-

ciple shows that "emphasis on large-scale industry with a high capital-output ratio as opposed to smaller, labor-intensive production
does not promote the optimal distribution of
resources in time and may actually slow down
the rate of economic progress" (p. 297).

The basic weakness of the position of Fei and
Ranis on this question — and they themselves
feel this — is that the "rapid employment
growth rate (absorption of the labor force) is
selected as the only criterion for "successful
developmental planning" (p. 297). "Many planning commission workers," the authors write,
"may not agree with this, in turn maintaining
that the proper criterion is increasing the industrial output and saying that they are ready
to sacrifice the 'more remote' goal of increasing employment in the name of this 'more pressing' goal.... In other words, everyone feels that
there is a conflict between maximum output and
maximum employment and that the latter must
be (and this is actually what happens) sacri-
ficed" (pp. 297-298). The authors try to show
that there is no unsolvable contradiction between
these two criteria.

The authors claim that the same factors determine both the growth rate of employment and
the growth rate of output. These factors are:
capital accumulation η_k and activities connected
with the innovation of existing production J, B_L:

a) $\eta_y = \eta_k + J(1 + \Phi_l/\varepsilon_{le}) + B_L(\Phi_l/\varepsilon_{le})^1,$
b) $\eta_l = \eta_k + J/\varepsilon_{le} + B_L/\varepsilon_{le}$ (17) (4)

with

$$J \geqslant 0,$$
$$\Phi_l > 0,$$
$$\varepsilon_{le} > 0,$$

where $\eta_y \left(\equiv \frac{dy}{dt} \Big/ y \right)$ is the output growth rate;
η_l is the employment growth rate; and
$\Phi_l \left(\equiv \frac{dy}{dL} \Big/ L \Big/ y \right)$ is the coefficient of elasticity of
the "labor-output" ratio (or the coefficient of
change in the share of labor in output).

Despite the fact that η_y and η_l are determined

by the same parameters, their maximum is attained in various points. The idea of the authors is that by using different variants, by partially sacrificing the principle of optimality or η_y or η_1, it is possible to bring these two points closer together — the maximum of output and the maximum of employment. This would be the optimal solution of the problem. We can see that such a solution of the problem of "labor-intensive versus capital-intensive production" is not very convincing. The advancement of maximum output as a basic criterion poses an essentially new problem.

In the process of development, the CMEC principle undergoes modification. After a certain turning point, when the "agricultural reserve army" is drained off and absorbed by industry, the price of the labor force begins to rise steadily (up to that point, as the authors believe, owing to the unlimited supply of manpower, wages were held at an unchanging level). Then the equation of employment growth rate 1 assumes the form

$$\eta_l = \eta_k + \frac{J + B_L}{\varepsilon_{le}} - \eta_w / \varepsilon_{le},$$

where $\eta_w \equiv \left(\frac{dw}{dt} \middle/ w \right)$ is the growth rate of real wages in time.

Accordingly, the equation of the growth rate of the "capital-labor" ratio assumes the form

$$\eta_q = \eta_w / \varepsilon_{le} - (J + B_L) / \varepsilon_{le}.$$

The use of the latest technology attained in developed countries, after labor has become a limited resource (reduction, in this connection, in magnitudes J and B_L, growth η_w, and other factors, at the given stage in the development of society leads to growth of η_q or to the utilization of technological modes with an ever higher capital-output ratio. In support of this idea, the authors once again cite the example of Japan, where, until World War I, the CMEC principle was implemented and wages increased to a very small extent, while after the war the second stage of development began with all its features,

in particular, a considerable growth in real wages (p. 305).

A statistical experiment by Fei and Ranis is given in the table data on pages 68, 69, and 70.

Advocating the criterion of employment as the basic criterion for capital investment during the formative stage of industry, Fei and Ranis are guided by a very weighty historical precedent (Japan). But without a comprehensive analysis of the process of economic growth in Japan, in our estimation, it is impossible to say for certain whether a given factor — growth of employment in Japanese industry during 1888-1930 — is one of the causes or simply an "accompanying circumstance" of the rapid industrial development of the nation during this period. The use of employment criterion as a basic criterion in the given context means placing emphasis on production with a low capital-output ratio. But the question arises whether all use of labor-intensive production forms, whether all manner of employment would lead to the desired effect. The materials cited by the authors do not answer this basic question. At the same time, only concrete forms of production with a low level of mechanization in a certain combination with other (developed) forms can be useful for the national economy. In other words, Fei and Ranis did not answer the basic questions of just what is the principal criterion for the selection of the technological mode and how one should judge the national economic effectiveness of capital investments in one or another form of production.

* * *

Thus, the basic criteria proposed by foreign authors can be united into three groups:

1. Net product (national income) per unit of capital investment. This criterion can be varied, can be complicated by various additional conditions (Chenery's effect on balance of payments, etc.). This criterion is most actively supported by Western economists.

2. Surplus product. Of the authors examined by us, Galenson and Leibenstein were most con-

Japan

	Analysis of CMEC principle (thousands of persons)			Analysis of production costs (million yen)		Analysis of component parts of employment growth (thousands of persons)		
Year	Total population. In parentheses: g	Employment in industry. In parentheses: ηl	Employment in agriculture. In parentheses: ηla	Capital K	"Capital-labor" ratio $K/L = q\Delta$ In parentheses: ηq	$\Delta L/\Delta t$ In parentheses: ηl	$\Delta r/\Delta t$ In parentheses: ηr	$\Delta h/\Delta t$ In parentheses: ηh
1	2	3	4	5	6	7	8	9
1888	39,362	4,993	17,050	21,331.8	4,272.34	—	—	—
1889	39,795 (1.10)	5,188 (3.90)	17,124 (0.43)	21,449.9	4,134.52 (−3.35)	195 (3.90)	24.5 (0.49)	170.5 (3.41)
1890	40,164 (0.93)	5,385 (3.80)	17,198 (0.43)	21,580.7	4,007.56 (−3.19)	197 (3.80)	28.6 (0.55)	168.4 (3.25)
1891	40,444 (0.70)	5,582 (3.66)	17,243 (0.26)	21,738.1	3,894.32 (−2.93)	197 (3.66)	32.7 (0.61)	164.3 (3.05)
1892	40,772 (0.81)	5,781 (3.57)	17,304 (0.35)	21,897.0	3,787.75 (−2.84)	199 (3.57)	37.3 (0.67)	161.7 (2.90)
1893	41,127 (0.87)	5,980 (3.44)	17,336 (0.18)	22,053.4	3,687.86 (−2.73)	199 (3.44)	41.7 (0.72)	157.3 (2.72)
1894	41,453 (0.79)	6,183 (3.39)	17,368 (0.18)	22,216.5	3,593.16 (−2.66)	203 (3.39)	47.3 (0.79)	155.7 (2.60)
1895	41,883 (1.04)	6,384 (3.25)	17,385 (0.10)	22,417.5	3,511.51 (−2.35)	201 (3.25)	51.7 (0.84)	149.3 (2.41)
1896	42,298 (0.99)	6,588 (3.20)	17,389 (0.02)	22,649.5	3,437.99 (−2.16)	204 (3.20)	57.5 (0.90)	146.5 (2.30)
1897	42,765 (1.10)	6,803 (3.26)	17,392 (0.02)	22,885.4	3,364.02 (−2.23)	215 (3.26)	66.3 (1.00)	148.7 (2.26)
1898	43,275 (1.19)	7,000 (2.90)	17,382 (−0.06)	23,152.2	3,307.46 (−1.72)	197 (2.90)	66.0 (0.97)	131.0 (1.93)
1899	43,736 (1.07)	7,216 (3.09)	17,356 (−0.15)	23,439.2	3,248.23 (−1.85)	216 (3.09)	78.1 (1.12)	137.9 (1.97)
1900	44,231 (1.13)	7,437 (3.06)	17,331 (−0.14)	23,697.7	3,186.46 (−1.96)	221 (3.06)	86.3 (1.20)	134.7 (1.87)

1	2	3	4	5	6	7	8	9
1901	44,748 (1.17)	7,666 (3.08)	17,293 (−0.22)	23,962.6	3,125.83 (−1.96)	229 (3.08)	96.4 (1.30)	132.6 (1.78)
1902	45,401 (1.46)	7,883 (2.83)	17,239 (−0.31)	24,242.5	3,075.29 (−1.66)	217 (2.83)	97.9 (1.28)	119.1 (1.55)
1903	45,988 (1.29)	8,111 (2.89)	17,187 (−0.30)	24,520.0	3,023.06 (−1.75)	228 (2.89)	109.8 (1.39)	118.2 (1.50)
1904	46,499 (1.11)	8,331 (2.96)	17,105 (−0.48)	24,821.9	2,979.46 (−1.73)	240 (2.96)	123.0 (1.52)	117.0 (1.44)
1905	46,934 (0.94)	8,561 (2.52)	17,038 (−0.39)	25,130.4	2,935.45 (−1.28)	210 (2.52)	114.1 (1.37)	95.9 (1.15)
1906	47,322 (0.83)	8,787 (2.64)	16,942 (−0.56)	25,480.8	2,899.83 (1.25)	226 (2.64)	129.9 (1.52)	96.1 (1.12)
1907	47,828 (1.07)	9,012 (2.56)	16,846 (−0.57)	25,842.7	2,867.59 (−1.14)	225 (2.56)	136.3 (1.55)	88.7 (1.01)
1908	48,407 (1.21)	9,234 (2.46)	16,737 (−0.65)	26,245.4	2,842.26 (−0.91)	222 (2.46)	141.4 (1.57)	80.6 (0.89)
1909	49,027 (1.28)	9,458 (2.43)	16,627 (−0.66)	26,730.4	2,826.22 (−0.58)	224 (2.43)	149.5 (1.62)	74.5 (0.81)
1910	49,685 (1.34)	9,680 (2.35)	16,489 (−0.83)	27,246.9	2,814.76 (−0.41)	222 (2.35)	155.0 (1.64)	67.0 (0.71)
1911	50,396 (1.43)	9,907 (2.34)	16,352 (−0.83)	27,792.9	2,805.38 (−0.34)	227 (2.35)	165.4 (1.71)	61.6 (0.64)
1912	51,123 (1.44)	10,134 (2.29)	16,213 (−0.85)	28,341.4	2,796.66 (−0.32)	227 (2.29)	172.3 (1.74)	54.7 (0.55)
1913	51,856 (1.43)	10,360 (2.23)	16,062 (−0.93)	28,897.4	2,789.32 (−0.27)	226 (2.23)	178.4 (1.76)	47.6 (0.47)
1914	52,574 (1.38)	10,590 (2.22)	15,881 (−1.13)	29,427.0	2,778.75 (−0.39)	230 (2.22)	188.4 (1.82)	41.6 (0.40)
1915	53,310 (1.40)	10,811 (2.09)	15,716 (−1.04)	30,001.4	2,775.08 (−0.14)	221 (2.09)	187.5 (1.77)	33.5 (0.32)
1916	53,975 (1.25)	11,036 (2.08)	15,521 (−1.24)	30,458.1	2,768.04 (−0.26)	225 (2.08)	197.3 (1.82)	27.7 (0.26)
1917	54,588 (1.15)	11,263 (2.05)	15,236 (−1.26)	31,189.5	2,769.20 (0.06)	227 (2.05)	205.6 (1.86)	21.4 (0.19)
1918	54,960 (0.86)	11,486 (1.98)	15,132 (−1.28)	31,926.5	2,779.61 (0.38)	223 (1.98)	208.2 (1.85)	14.8 (0.13)
1919	55,363 (0.73)	11,714 (1.99)	14,901 (−1.53)	32,673.3	2,789.25 (0.35)	228 (1.99)	219.1 (1.91)	8.9 (0.08)

Japan (continued)

1	2	3	4	5	6	7	8	9
1920	55,944	12,415	14,848	33,453.7	2,694.62	701	712.5	−11.5
	(1.05)	(5.98)	(−0.36)		(−3.59)	(5.98)	(6.08)	(−0.10)
1921	56,624	12,663	14,835	34,527.1	2,726.61	248	343.8	−95.8
	(1.22)	(2.00)	(−0.09)		(1.21)	(2.00)	(2.77)	(−0.77)
1922	57,357	12,910	14,823	35,630.1	2,759.88	247	363.9	−116.9
	(1.29)	(1.95)	(−0.09)		(1.24)	(1.95)	(2.87)	(−0.92)
1923	58,331	13,159	14,810	36,651.3	2,785.26	249	387.6	−138.6
	(1.70)	(1.93)	(−0.09)		(0.94)	(1.93)	(3.00)	(−1.07)
1924	58,864	13,409	14,797	37.677.5	2,809.87	250	409.1	−159.1
	(0.91)	(1.90)	(−0.09)		(0.90)	(1.90)	(3.11)	(−1.21)
1925	59,757	13,657	14,785	38,781.6	2,839.69	248	424.6	−176.6
	(1.87)	(1.85)	(−0.08)		(1.08)	(1.85)	(3.17)	(−1.32)
1926	60,522	13,904	14,772	40,067.3	2,881.71	247	440.4	−193.4
	(1.28)	(1.81)	(−0.09)		(1.51)	(1.81)	(3.22)	(−1.42)
1927	61,317	14,153	14,760	41,423.9	2,926.86	249	460.7	−211.7
	(1.31)	(1.79)	(−0.08)		(1.60)	(1.79)	(3.31)	(−1.52)
1928	62,122	14,402	14,746	42,783.9	2,970.69	249	476.5	−227.5
	(1.31)	(1.76)	(−0.09)		(1.52)	(1.76)	(3.37)	(−1.61)
1929	62,938	14,650	14,734	44,093.9	3,009.82	248	489.2	−241.2
	(1.31)	(1.72)	(−0.08)		(1.34)	(1.72)	(3.40)	(−1.67)
1930	64,450	14,898	14,721	45,710.9	3,068.26	248	502.9	−245.9
	(2.40)	(1.69)	(−0.09)		(1.98)	(1.69)	(3.43)	(−1.74)

sistently in favor of this criterion.

3. Employment. Champions of this criterion are the most numerous, particularly in the developing countries themselves. A policy of capital investments that increases employment in many cases is actively supported by the ruling circles of these countries.

With respect to the methods of analysis used in the works we examined, it is possible to make a number of critical comments. In the first place, note should be made of the formal approach of most of the authors to the problem and the neglect of the most essential socioeconomic conditions in the economically underdeveloped countries. However, we have not set ourselves the task of making a detailed analysis of foreign works. We were primarily interested in the extent to which the problem of the effec-

tiveness of capital investments in modes of production with varying degrees of capital-intensiveness had been investigated, as well as how an approach had been established concerning the criterion of the effectiveness of these capital investments. It is our view that on the whole the criteria proposed above do not solve the problem even though this does not mean that individual mathematical constructs — in particular, those of Chenery and Sen — cannot be used for further elaboration. We shall examine the basic shortcomings of the proposed criteria.

Criterion 1 — the increase in national income per unit of capital investment. Does this criterion provide a solution to the problem of "capital-intensive versus labor-intensive production" under the conditions of a developing economy during the transitional period? In our opinion, it does not. Indeed, the maximization of national income under the specific conditions of one or another production unit means the maximum output of net product per unit of capital investment. In turn, the net product is a complex category that incorporates two components: variable capital and surplus value. If the goal is that of increasing net output without regard to time, then in many instances the choice will fall on small-scale production. The same holds true if the period during which it is proposed to obtain a full return on capital investment is not great. If we take a longer period, however, then the paramount importance is acquired by the size of the surplus value that can be used to expand production. Depending on our selection of one or another technological mode of production, maximization of the net product will in one case mean increasing employment (small-scale industry), while in another — growth of surplus product and accumulation fund (factory industry).

Accordingly, by selecting the volume of the national income per unit of capital investment as a basic criterion, we do not advance one iota in the solution of the problem of what we must increase — output or solely "surplus" for maximizing the growth rate. The task of increasing total income for some period may be posed. In this case, however, the duration of the period must be given, and this is not always practically possible. Moreover, the fulfillment of the task of maximizing output for an entire period does not always coincide with the requirement for a given product within this period. Such are the basic shortcomings of the "national income-capital" criterion.

Criterion 2 entails the selection of a technological mode that will guarantee the largest accumulation fund and, correspondingly, the most rapid growth rates for a given branch of industry. If the period during which it is proposed to realize an effect from capital investments is sufficiently extended, then the maximum growth rates of the surplus product will also guarantee a maximum return in the form of net product and maximum employment.

The basic shortcoming of this criterion is that it does not consider the specifics of developing countries, in particular, the existence of a large number of unemployed or partly employed able-bodied persons in them. In this connection, the selection always falls on the most capital-intensive modes of production, while the possibility of using such a mighty resource as the free labor force cannot be realized. Moreover, under this criterion, use is made of technology of the automated type of production unit, which is not only low in labor-intensiveness but even "economizes on labor," and under the conditions of the presently developing countries this is not always profitable in the broad sense of the word. If one takes this criterion to be the main and all-encompassing criterion, it may happen that the entire economy for some time will be forced sharply to decelerate the production rate and to curtail the overall volume of production until such time as the development of selected highly mechanized production modes yields a sufficiently high level of accumulation and thus provides the rapid rates of development for which the calculation was made.

Criterion 3 — maximum growth of employment. The study of the problem of increasing employment in a number of developing countries is unquestionably extremely important. Achieving a growth of employment that outstrips population growth and is an additional source for increasing the welfare of these countries is one of the most important tasks at the present time. It seems to us that it is precisely in this light that the problem of employment in developing countries must be generally formulated. It is also unquestionable, however, that employment must be an additional factor that stimulates capital investments and not the principal criterion of the effectiveness of capital investments. The use of employment growth as a basic criterion can lead to gross economic miscalculations or, as S. K. Basu, the Indian economist specializing in the field of small-scale industry, properly noted, "to the substitution of one kind of disguised unemployment and inefficiency by another."[18] The example concerning hand-

India

Year	Analysis of CMEC principle (thousands of persons)		Analysis of production costs (million rupees)		Analysis of component parts of employment growth (thousands of persons)		
	Total population. In parentheses: g	Employment in industry. In parentheses: l	Capital In parentheses: K	"Capital-labor" ratio $K/L = q$ In parentheses: ηq	$\Delta L/\Delta t$ In parentheses: ηl	$\Delta r/\Delta t$ In parentheses: ηr	$\Delta h/\Delta t$ In parentheses: ηh
1	2	3	4	5	6	7	8
1949	339,722	14,143	28.54	2,017.96	—	—	—
1950	348,195 (2.494)	14,476 (2.4)	29.14 (2.1)	2,012.99 (0.3)	333 (2.4)	297.3 (2.1)	35.7 (0.3)
1951	356,879 (2.494)	14,802 (2.3)	30.10 (3.3)	2,033.51 (1.0)	326 (2.3)	476.9 (3.3)	−150.9 (−1.0)
1952	365,776 (2.494)	15,062 (1.8)	30.66 (1.9)	2,035.59 (0.1)	260 (1.8)	275.4 (1.9)	−15.4 (−0.1)
1953	374,895 (2.494)	15,282 (1.5)	31.65 (3.2)	2,071.06 (1.7)	220 (1.5)	486.3 (3.2)	−266.3 (−1.7)
1954	384,241 (2.494)	15,546 (1.7)	32.67 (3.2)	2,101.51 (1.5)	264 (1.7)	455.0 (2.9)	−191.0 (−1.2)
1955	393,826 (2.494)	15,900 (2.3)	33.97 (4.0)	2,136.48 (1.7)	354 (2.3)	991.2 (6.4)	−637.2 (−4.1)
1956	401,574 (1.967)	16,721 (5.2)	37.97 (11.8)	2,270.80 (6.6)	821 (5.2)	3,668.9 (23.1)	−2,847.9 (−17.9)
1957	409,322 (1.929)	16,899 (1.1)	41.08 (8.2)	2,430.91 (7.1)	178 (1.1)	964.9 (5.8)	−7,864.0 (−4.7)
1958	417,071 (1.823)	16,999 (0.6)	45.17 (10.0)	2,657.22 (9.4)	100 (0.6)	561.0 (3.3)	−461.0 (−2.7)
1959	424,819 (1.858)	17,183 (1.1)	49.09 (8.7)	2,856.89 (7.6)	184 (1.1)	1,063.1 (6.3)	−879.1 (−5.2)
1960	432,567 (1.823)	17,255 (0.4)	53.19 (8.4)	3,082.58 (8.0)	72 (0.4)	425.2 (2.5)	−353.2 (−2.1)

spinning in India has already been mentioned above. Evidently there are numerous such examples. In some cases, the inefficiency of the technological modes of production is obvious even if they do promise high employment. For example, no one would seriously consider using a toy scoop shovel to dig wells no matter how much employment these "modes of production" promise in the face of limited capital. In other cases, however, it is more difficult to reveal this ineffectiveness if the sole guideline is the criterion of employment.

Under the present conditions of the developing countries, increasing employment by selecting a more labor-intensive production mode almost always means an increase in consumption at the expense of accumulation. Therefore, an increase in employment for an immediate period is by no means adequate to an increase in employment for some extended period. Accordingly, the problem once more arises of selecting a period during which it is proposed to realize the effect from capital investments and of selecting, in accordance with this period, either the technological modes maximizing output (as a rule, these will be modes that immediately increase employment) or modes that maximize the surplus product and the accumulation fund. In this case, employment will grow less rapidly than in the first case during the initial period. After a certain critical period of time, however, employment will increase at a more rapid rate.

From the above brief survey of the works of foreign authors we can conclude that investigations of the criteria of capital investment effectiveness, conducted in isolation from the concrete economic situation, are somewhat reminiscent of the search for the "philosopher's stone." Therein lies one of the chief shortcomings of the examined studies.

Footnotes

1) The term "capital-intensiveness" ["kapitaloemkost' "] denotes the magnitude of the "capital-output" ratio, but for the sake of convenience we shall more frequently use the reverse ratio — "output-capital."

2) Gustav Ranis, "Investment Criteria, Productivity and Economic Development: An Empirical Comment," The Quarterly Journal of Economics, Vol. LXXVI, No. 2, May 1962, p. 298.

3) D. T. Lakdawala and J. C. Sandesara, Small Industry in a Big City. A Survey in Bombay, Bombay, 1960, p. 4.

4) Alfred E. Kahn, "Investment Criteria in Development Programs," The Quarterly Journal of Economics, Vol. LXV, No. 1, February 1951.

5) H. B. Chenery. "The Application of Investment Criteria," The Quarterly Journal of Economics, February 1953.

6) Ibid.

7) Economically underdeveloped regions of these countries are examined.

8) H. B. Chenery and P. Clark, Ekonomika mezhotraslevykh sviazei, Moscow, 1962, p. 316.

9) W. Galenson and H. Leibenstein, "Investment Criteria, Productivity and Economic Development," The Quarterly Journal of Economics, Vol. LXIX, No. 3, August 1955.

10) A. K. Sen, Choice of Techniques. An Aspect of the Theory of Planned Economic Development, Oxford, 1960.

11) R. Balakrishna, Review of Economic Growth in India, Bangalore, 1961. The author is Professor of Economics at Madras University.

12) Lakdawala and Sandesara, op. cit.

13) Eva Garzouzi, Old Ills and New Remedies in Egypt, Cairo (1967).

14) With reference to The Second Five-Year Plan (India), p. 114: K. N. Kaj, "Small-Scale Industries, Problems of Technological Change," Economic Weekly, April 7 and 14, 1956.

15) Baljit Singh, The Economics of Small-Scale Industries. A Case Study of Small-Scale Industrial Establishments of Moradabad, Bombay, 1961.

16) John C. H. Fei and Gustav Ranis, Innovation, Capital Accumulation and Economic Development, Yale University Economic Growth Center, Paper No. 22, New Haven (Connecticut), 1963.

17) Derived by differentiating the function $Y = f(K, L, t)$ with respect to t.

18) S. K. Basu, Place and Problems of Small Industries, Calcutta, 1957, p. 86.

CHAPTER V

The Problem of Effectiveness and Planning of Capital Investments in Various Technological Modes of Production

In the preceding chapters we examined the most important indicators of productive activity of two types of industrial production that are different in their degree of capital-intensiveness: small-scale industry with a low level of mechanization, and the highly mechanized factory industry. Let us once more summarize our basic observations. With respect to the indicators of interest to us — the size of gross product, of value added, and of the surplus product per unit of invested capital — the basic industrial branches of developing countries may be divided into three groups: (1) branches in which small-scale production has higher indicators of gross output and value added per unit of capital as compared with factory production, but has a lower profit norm; (2) branches in which small-scale industry has higher indicators both for gross output and value added as well as for profit norm; (3) branches where, on the contrary, the factory industry has higher indicators in these respects.

Clearly, for purposes of the present investigation it is the first group of branches that is of the greatest interest, because the situation with the other two groups is clear: in the first instance, all the advantages are on the side of small-scale industry and it has every right to priority capital investments, while in the second instance factory industry has an undivided claim to the entire possible investment sum.

The problem of planning capital investment in enterprises of the first group of branches is the most complex one and requires a special approach for its solution. Because the first group of branches is the most widespread in the developing countries, this very problem is of vitally important and not merely academic interest.

As the materials show, the choice of small-scale industry in the first group of branches as an object of capital investments yields a maximum growth of output only if a limited time period is involved. Beyond this time period, owing to higher rates of capital accumulation, the product becomes maximized in the factory industry, while small-scale production begins to lag farther and farther behind.

We shall illustrate this on the basis of one of the branches in India's manufacturing industry (see Table 8). In order to simplify the calculations, we shall assume that both in small-scale and factory industry, the entire surplus product is invested annually ($I = S = m$, where I is investment; S is accumulation; and m is the branch's surplus product). It is assumed that there is no time lag in putting the investment into operation.

As the table shows, during the first five years the small enterprises produce more gross and net product on the invested capital than the corresponding factory enterprises. After five years,

Table 8

India. Dynamics of Growth of Basic Economic Indicators Calculated in Terms of the Fixed Initial Sum of Capital Investments in Factory and Small-Scale Industry

(light machine-building; rupees)

Time (years)	Factory industry					Small-scale industry				
	K	V	m $\left(\frac{m}{K}=0.39\right)$	P $\left(\frac{P}{K}=1.75\right)$	y $\left(\frac{y}{K}=0.82\right)$	K	V	m $\left(\frac{m}{K}=.33\right)$	P $\left(\frac{P}{K}=3.06\right)$	y $\left(\frac{y}{K}=1.03\right)$
1	6,290	2,705	2,453	11,000	5,158	6,290	4,403	2,076	19,247	6,479
2	8,743	3,759	3,410	15,300	7,169	8,366	5,856	2,761	25,600	8,617
3	12,153	5,225	4,740	21,268	9,965	11,127	7,789	3,672	34,049	11,461
4	16,893	7,264	6,588	29,563	13,852	14,799	10,359	4,884	45,285	15,243
5	23,481	10,096	9,158	41,092	19,254	19,683	13,778	6,495	60,230	20,273
6	32,639	14,035	12,729	57,118	26,764	26,178	18,264	8,639	80,105	26,903
7	45,368	19,508	17,694	79,394	37,202	34,817	24,372	11,490	106,540	35,862
8	63,062	27,116	24,594	110,358	51,710	46,307	32,415	15,281	141,699	47,696
9	87,656	37,692	34,186	153,378	71,878	61,588	43,112	20,324	188,459	63,436
10	121,842	52,392	47,518	213,224	99,910	81,912	57,338	27,031	250,651	84,369
11	169,360	72,825	66,050	296,380	138,875	108,943	76,260	35,951	333,366	112,211
12	235,410	101,226	91,810	411,968	193,036	144,894	101,426	47,815	443,376	149,241
13	327,220	140,604	127,716	572,635	268,320	192,709	134,896	53,594	589,689	198,490
14	454,936	195,623	177,425	796,138	373,048	256,303	179,412	84,580	784,287	263,992
15	632,361	271,915	246,621	1,106,632	518,536	340,883	238,618	112,491	1,043,102	351,109

Compiled on the basis of data in Table 3.

more net product is produced in factory industry, although for gross product small-scale industry is still in the lead. In the fourteenth year,
factory industry begins to outstrip small-scale
industry in its gross output as well. Thus, for
each indicator one can find a critical point where
one or another technological mode yields its advantage to another. The longer the investment
planning period, moreover, the greater the
probability that the most favorable results will
be demonstrated by factory industry. This can
be shown on a graph where lines A and B represent output in the factory and small-scale industry, respectively (Fig. 2).

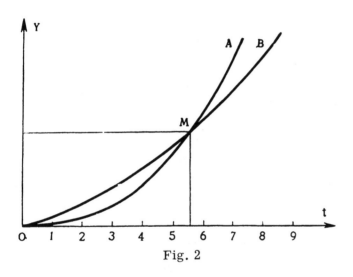

Fig. 2

The complexity of choosing among various
technological modes is that it is impossible to
choose any one of them such that there would be
a maximum growth both in the size of the output
and of the surplus product. We remind the
reader that this refers to branches in the above-
defined first group. We shall examine this in a
graph.

A number of technological modes of production differing in degree of labor-intensiveness
(with a given size of capital) are given on the
horizontal axis. Along the vertical axis are the volumes of net output corresponding to these modes.
Because branches in the first group are being
examined, the function characterizing changes
in output depending on the capital-intensiveness
of the technological mode will be of the form
shown in the figure. Function Y(x) will be convex

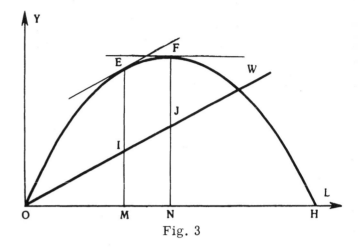

Fig. 3

upward (an increase in output on one and the
same invested capital in proportion to increases
in the labor-intensiveness of the process) and
nonlinear; it is described by the equation

$$Y(x) = C_0 + C_1 x + \ldots + C_n x^n.$$

Curve OEFH, representing function Y(x), increases upward to a certain point (maximum F),
after which, notwithstanding further increases
in labor-intensiveness, it tends toward zero
(less and less effective replacement of capital
by labor). Segments OF and FH are not necessarily symmetrical, i.e., a decrease in output
after point F may occur more rapidly or more
slowly than the increase in output to point F.
The line OW — the wage fund, which, according
to our assumption, is proportional to employment — divides segments EM and FN into two
parts: MI, NJ (necessary product) and EI, FJ
(surplus product). The maximum output is
reached at point F, the maximum surplus product at point E.

Because certain foreign scholars try to solve
the "capital intensive-labor intensive production" problem by finding the point of con-
vergence of both maxima (e.g., Fei and Ranis),
we shall see whether this is possible for the
function of the given type and under what conditions.

We shall determine the position of points F
and E — maxima Y(x) and m(x), respectively.

Maximum Y(x) is reached at point x_1, where

$$\left. \frac{dY}{dx} \right|_{x=x_1} = 0 . \qquad (*)$$

The derivative equals 0 at the point whose tangent is parallel to the axis of the abscissa (the inclination of the tangent line = 0).

Surplus product m(x) is determined by the expression

$$m(x) = Y(x) - W(x), \qquad (**)$$

and under the assumption of the linearity of the wage function

$$W(x) = x \cdot \mathrm{tg}\,\alpha. \qquad (***)$$

The maximum of function m(x) is reached at point x_2:

$$\left.\frac{dm}{dx}\right|_{x=x_2} = 0.$$

Considering expressions (**) and (***), we find

$$\frac{dm}{dx} = \frac{dY}{dx} - \frac{dW}{dx} = \left.\frac{dY}{dx}\right|_{x=x_2} - \mathrm{tg}\,\alpha. \qquad (****)$$

Under what conditions does $x_1 = x_2 = x^*$, i.e., do points E and F coincide? From expressions (*) and (***) we obtain

$$\left.\frac{dY}{dx}\right|_{x=x^*} = \left.\frac{dY}{dx}\right|_{x=x^*} - \mathrm{tg}\,\alpha = 0.$$

From this it follows: $\mathrm{tg}\,\alpha = 0$, which is equivalent to W(x) = 0.

Thus, the maxima of functions Y(x) and m(x) coincide when W(x) = 0, or when the line OW coincides with the axis of the abscissa. In economic terms this means that the maximum growth of output and the maximum growth of surplus value coincide provided that outlays on wages are equal to zero, and this, in practice, is impossible. From the foregoing it is also evident that even though maxima E and F cannot entirely coincide, nonetheless with a decline in the wage level (decrease in angle α) maximum m(x) (point E) will approach point F.

Let us now examine the general relationships among gross output, the volumes of the net product, and surplus product, and capital.

The basic indicators are interconnected in the following way:

$$\begin{aligned}
P_t &= Y_t + X_t, \\
Y_t &= V_t + S_t, \\
P &= a \cdot K, \\
Y &= b \cdot K, \\
X &= (a - b) \cdot K, \\
m &= p' \cdot K,
\end{aligned}$$

where P_t is gross output in year t; Y_t is net output; X_t is outlays on constant capital (dimensions of the transferred value); V_t represents outlays on variable capital (wages); S_t — size of accumulation in year t; m — surplus product; a = P/K — "gross output-capital" ratio; b = Y/K — "net output-capital" ratio; and p' = m/K — "surplus product-capital" ratio (profit norm).

Making the following assumptions: $S_t = m_t$, i.e., the entire sum of the surplus value produced is invested, and coefficients a and b are constant, we see that changes in P, Y, and m are connected exclusively with a change in K. For the case when there is no lag in the putting into operation of new capital investments and accumulation takes the form of capital at the end of the time interval (i.e., accumulations created in year t − 1 participate completely in production during year t), the formula for capital increase will be of the form:

$$K_t = K_0 (1 + p')^{t-1}.$$

Hence,

$$\begin{aligned}
P_t &= a K_0 (1 + p')^{t-1}, \\
Y_t &= b K_0 (1 + p')^{t-1}, \\
m_t &= p' K_0 (1 + p')^{t-1}.
\end{aligned}$$

Now it is necessary to introduce time lags in our equations. We shall denote the time necessary for the putting into operation of capital investments by l(l = 1, 2, 3, ... n). Moreover, for the sake of simplicity we shall agree that the lags have equal intervals and are uniform for all parts of the invested capital. In this case, the formula for compound interest that we used to calculate increase in capital is no longer usable. The investment fund (capital in operation + capital investments not in operation), under our assumption, being equal to the entire sum of the surplus product produced up to t-th year in year t, constitutes

$$I_t = K_t + S_t,$$

where K_t is capital in operation; S_t is the surplus product produced at a given time (capital investments not in operation) or

$$S_t = \sum_{i-l}^{t} m.$$

The capital in operation in year t equals

$$K_t = I_{t-l}.$$

The practical calculation of it, however, is difficult in this form. In order to find the capital that is in operation in year t, we shall apply the recurrent relationship

$$K_t = K_{t-1} + p' \cdot K_{t-1-l}.$$

With the aid of K_t, which is found in this way, and parameters a, b, and p', P_t (output in year t), Y_t (net product) and m_t (surplus product) are calculated.

The introduction of time lags in putting capital into operation considerably changes the picture, in this case in favor of small-scale industry. In the case of lags, the effect from capital investments naturally is as if extended over a longer period (see Table 9). The first critical point at which production by the two technological modes is at the same level appears in the ninth year in our concrete example (net output). The critical point for gross output occurs still later.

Up to now we have proceeded from the assumption that parameters a, b, and p' are constant. As a matter of fact, this is the same assumption made by all foreign authors studying this problem. If one takes a brief historical period, there is no great error in this assumption, because the enumerated coefficients, particularly a and b, are relatively slow in changing. However, for long-term planning for, let

us say, several five-year plans as is done in India, the use of constant parameters can lead to considerable inaccuracies. Therefore, the given parameters must be made variable.

Below is one of the directions for the solution of this problem:

$$a = a_0 + \overline{a},$$

$$b = b_0 + \overline{b},$$

$$p' = p'_0 + \overline{p}'.$$

Here, a_0, b_0, and p'_0, are initial values of coefficients supposed to be constant; $\overline{a}$, $\overline{b}$, $\overline{p}'$ are the variable parts of the respective coefficients. Accordingly, $P_t = (a_0 + \overline{a}) \cdot K_t$, etc.

The magnitude of changes in coefficient a depends on the following basic factors:

(a) technical progress, as a result of which labor productivity may increase with a non-proportional increase in the capital-output ratio;

(b) introduction of new technology in other branches;

(c) innovation in production without increasing its capital-intensiveness;

(d) measures of a nationwide nature (e.g., nationalization of land), changing the value of fixed capital and, accordingly, the "output-capital" ratio with the same output level.

Clearly, a quantitative assessment of these factors can only be made on the basis of a large body of statistical material. The method of selection and comparison of the operation of these factors on the basis of the historical materials of the developed countries is entirely acceptable in the first approximation. This is a big job which still remains to be done.

For practical purposes, the sequence of work involving coefficient $\overline{a}$ could be as follows:

if a brief historical period is taken (let us say, 5-10 years), then $\overline{a}$ can practically be neglected;

for a longer period (e.g., up to 15 years), in our view, it is sufficient to use average indicators of changes in $\overline{a}$, adduced with the aid of

Table 9

India. Dynamics of Growth of Basic Economic Indicators Calculated in Terms of the Fixed Initial Sum of Capital Investments with a Time Lag of One Year in Putting Capital into Operation

(light machine-building; rupees)

Time (years)	Factory industry						Small-scale industry					
	I_t		V	m $\left(\frac{m}{K}=0.39\right)$	P $\left(\frac{P}{K}=1.75\right)$	Y $\left(\frac{Y}{K}=0.82\right)$	I_t		V	m $\left(\frac{m}{K}=0.33\right)$	P $\left(\frac{P}{K}=3.06\right)$	Y $\left(\frac{Y}{K}=1.03\right)$
	K_t	S_t					K_t	S_t				
1	6,290	—	2,705	2,453	11,000	5,158	6,290	—	4,403	2,076	19,247	6,479
2	6,290	2,453	2,705	2,453	11,008	5,158	6,290	2,076	4,403	2,076	19,247	6,479
3	8,743	2,453	3,759	3,410	15,300	7,169	8,366	2,076	5,857	2,760	25,600	8,617
4	11,196	3,410	4,816	4,366	19,593	9,181	10,442	2,760	7,309	3,446	31,953	10,755
5	14,606	4,366	6,281	5,696	25,560	11,977	13,202	3,446	9,242	4,356	40,398	13,598
6	18,972	5,696	8,158	7,399	33,201	15,557	16,648	4,356	11,654	5,493	50,942	17,147
7	24,668	7,399	10,607	9,621	43,169	20,228	21,004	5,493	14,703	6,931	64,272	21,634
8	32,067	9,621	13,789	12,506	56,117	26,295	26,497	6,931	18,547	8,744	81,081	27,291
9	41,688	12,506	17,926	16,258	72,954	34,184	33,428	8,744	23,399	11,031	102,290	34,430
10	54,194	16,258	23,303	21,136	94,839	44,439	42,172	11,031	29,520	13,917	129,046	43,437
11	70,452	21,136	30,294	27,476	123,291	57,770	53,203	13,917	37,242	17,557	162,801	54,799
12	91,588	27,476	39,383	35,719	160,279	75,102	61,720	17,557	43,302	20,367	188,883	63,571
13	119,064	35,719	51,197	46,435	208,362	97,632	79,277	20,367	55,505	26,161	242,588	81,655
14	154,783	46,435	66,557	60,365	270,870	126,922	105,438	26,161	73,806	34,795	322,640	108,601
15	201,218	60,365	86,524	78,475	352,131	164,999	131,599	34,795	99,119	43,428	402,692	135,547

Compiled on the basis of data in Table 3.

statistical material on underdeveloped and developed countries;

in planning for a still more extended period, these calculations will be too gross and it will be necessary to investigate $\bar{a}$ more carefully as a function of several variables:

$$\bar{a} = \mathfrak{f}(x,\ y,\ z\ \ldots),$$

where x, y, z... are corresponding factors influencing changes in the "output-capital" coefficient.

Approximately the same factors influence changes in coefficient b.

More dynamic than the above-named coefficients is the profit norm indicator. This is explained by the fact that unlike "output-capital" and "net output-capital" ratios, the profit norm is connected not only with the production sphere but also with the circulation sphere. Therefore, coefficient p_c', even with the calculated correction p', will always be only a very approximate, average indicator. Of the basic factors determining changes in p', the following can be singled out:

(a) changes in the organic composition of capital;

(b) increases in the degree of labor exploitation as a result of the application of more productive technology, intensification of the labor process, innovation in production;

(c) "pulling" wages in production with low levels of mechanization up to the "normal" level, i.e., to the level of wages in factory industry;

(d) a certain lowering of the profit norm as a result of the gradual saturation of the internal market with industrial commodities.

In our opinion, the solution of the problem of the variable coefficient p' also lies in the investigation of a complex function of several arguments. The simplest form of this function has already been cited above:

$$p' = m'\ \frac{V}{K}\ ,$$

where m′ is the norm of surplus value, and V/K is the expression reflecting the level of the organic composition of capital.

One of the most important questions in determining the effectiveness of capital investments is that of evaluating outlays and receipts of foreign currency as a result of investment. According to Chenery's formula, which evaluates the effectiveness of capital investments in various projects, the aggregate effect of capital investments on the balance of payments "is added to the overall effect": (1)

$$SMP = \left(\frac{V}{K}\right) \cdot \left(\frac{V-C}{V}\right) + \frac{rB}{K}\ ,$$

where B is the aggregate effect on the balance of payments, and r is the coefficient covering the difference in the purchasing power of currencies.

In the aggregate effect on the balance of payments, Chenery isolates a number of the most important factors. The effect of investment period B_1 is influenced by:

(1) the purchase of machines and equipment abroad;

(2) the multiplier effect of investments on income and imports.

The direct operational effect B_2' is influenced by:

(3) output that increases exports or replaces imports;

(4) imports (direct or indirect) for the production of a given product;

(5) curtailment of the need for imports for the production of goods in connection with the production of item X as a substitute.

Indirect operational effect B_2'' is determined by:

(6) the multiplier effect of inflationary financing of consumption;

(7) the multiplier effect from changes in the size of the export (import) surplus.

Of these factors, the third factor is always positive, while factors 1, 2, 4, and 6 are always negative; factors 5 and 7 may be either positive or negative. (2)

The formula of the effect of the investment period is:

$$B_1 = -m_l K - mz\,(1-m_l)\,K,$$

where m_i is the portion of the investments requiring imports (direct or indirect); m is the relationship between an increase in imports and a growth in national income; z is the coefficient that takes into account the multiplier effect from the growth in imports.

The formula of the direct operational effect is:

$$B_2' = e(1-\overline{m}_p)X - c\overline{m}_pX + g(\overline{m}_p' - \overline{m}_p)X,$$

where e is the part of the output that goes into exports or into replacing imports; c is the part of the output that goes to expand internal consumption; g is the part of the output that replaces previously consumed commodities $e+g+c=1$; $\overline{m}_p$ is the ratio of the import of goods for productive consumption to output; $\overline{m}_p'$ is the ratio of new output replacing the import of goods for productive consumption to output.

The formula for indirect operational effect is:

$$B_2'' = -mzf(1-\overline{m}_p)X - mzB_2',$$

where f is the portion of the output that is financed by inflationary sums.

By using the formulas of the effect of the investment period and of the direct and indirect operational effects, we obtain a formula for the aggregate effect on the balance of payments:

$$\frac{B}{K} = -am_i - amz(1-m_i) + \frac{X}{K}[eu(1-\overline{m}_p) - cu\overline{m}_p + gu(\overline{m}_p' - \overline{m}_p) - mzf(1-\overline{m}_p)],$$

where a represents total payments for loans and interest on the loans, $u = (1-mz)$, (3) or, in abbreviated form:

$$B = aB_1 + B_2' + B_2''.$$

In our estimation, Chenery's formulas define with sufficient completeness the effect of capital investments on the balance of payments and are on the whole suitable for practical purposes. Chenery himself recommends these formulas principally for comparing various projects in various branches. It seems to us, however, that they can also be used for comparing the effectiveness of various technological modes. Here, the only requirement is that the initially invested capital be identical. We shall examine two particular cases for the latter formula.

First case. The production of a branch is intended entirely for internal consumption (e = 0, g = 0, c = 1). The formula acquires the following form:

$$\frac{B}{K} = -a[m_i + mz(1-m_i)] - \frac{X}{K}\overline{m}_pu.$$

In this case the effect will be entirely negative; and comparison of various technological modes should show which of them will entail the least loss from this point of view.

Second case. Capital investments go entirely to export branches (e = 1, g = 0, c = 0). Then

$$\frac{B}{K} = -a[m_i + mz(1-m_i)] + \frac{X}{K}(1-\overline{m}_p)u.$$

We shall denote the first member of the right-hand side of the equation by X; the second — by Y. It is assumed that the foreign currency effect of already operative capital investments (let us say, the results of the first year following the investment realization period) is being evaluated. The following variants are possible:

$$X > Y; \ X = Y; \ X < Y.$$

It is clear that in planning the creation of export branches we can be interested only in the latter variant when X < Y. Other variants are simply discarded as inexpedient. Accordingly, the effect of capital investments on the balance of payments in this case must be strictly positive. Comparison of various technological modes according to this indicator has the goal of eliciting the mode giving the greatest effect or the maximum positive number B/K.

For determining parameter r, use may be made of the formula for the volume of export necessary for the acquisition of Sen's corresponding import unit. This formula, which considers changes in foreign trade prices in connection with changing supply and demand (elasticity of supply and demand), is of the form: (4)

$$X = \frac{F\left(1 + \frac{1}{e}\right)}{G(1 - h)},$$

where X is the amount of export necessary for the acquisition of a unit of import; F is the value of the unit of import; G is the value of the unit of export; e is the elasticity of supply for a given import commodity; and h is the elasticity of demand for export commodities.

The coefficient of elasticity is defined as

$$\frac{\Delta q}{q + \Delta q} \Big/ \frac{\Delta p}{p}, \text{ i.e.,}$$

$$\frac{\text{change in quantity of product}}{\text{final quantity of product}} \Big/ \frac{\text{changes in price}}{\text{initial price}}$$

Considering the effect on the balance of payments, the formula for the gross product at time t will assume the form

$$P_t = aK_t - (r-1) B^0_{t-1} + (r-1) B_t.$$

where B^0_{t-1} is the effect on the balance of payments during the investment period (factors 1 and 2, under the above classification). For every t, this period will be $t-1$; B_t is the effect on the balance of payments during the operational period (factors 3 to 7).

$$B_t = (B'_t + B''_t),$$

where B'_t is the dimensions of the output increasing the export or replacing imports (positive effect); B''_t is the outlays of foreign currency in the process of producing a given item (negative effect) and r, as shown above, is determined according to Sen's formula.

The values of component B in our formula differ from the values of B in the above-cited formula of Chenery, even though essentially they represent only a certain regrouping of fac-

tors. This is for greater simplicity and convenience in the use of the formula. As before, the general value of B can be calculated according to Chenery's formula.

Formulas for the determination of the net product and surplus value at time t are written correspondingly.

K_t is determined either according to the formula $K_t = K_0 (1 + p')^{t-1}$ (in the absence of lags) or according to $K_t = K_{t-1} + p' \cdot K_{t-1-l}$ (in the case of time lag 1 in putting investments into operation).

Formulas permitting the determination of the size of the gross, net, and surplus product at a given moment for a fixed initial capital can serve as a practical instrument for comparing the economic possibilities of one or another mode of production. However, their importance is limited to this. They cannot answer the question posed at the beginning of the present work: what is the criterion or the criteria for using capital-intensive or labor-intensive production units and highly mechanized processes under the specific conditions of developing nations?

In our opinion, the selection of the criteria for capital investments in various technological modes of production is determined first and foremost by the complex of those economic and, in some cases, social conditions under which the decision must be made. We can imagine many different situations affecting the solution of this problem. Naturally, it is impossible to foresee them all. Presented below is one of the situations that, in our opinion, is most typical for the developing countries and the decision that might be made in this case.

Let us assume that the basic task in the economic policy of developing countries is that of securing the balanced growth of the national economy as a whole. (5) At the present time in these countries, however, it is frequently the case that even a single production facility — let us say, the chemical industry — is not entirely supplied with all components necessary to turn out the finished product. Sometimes these components are produced within the country, but not in sufficient quantity, and in other cases they are not produced at all. In order for the branch to function, these deficit components must be imported. Then the first task is that of ensuring the necessary volume of the gross product, of bringing the output of it to a level that will satisfy the demands of internal productive or mass consumption.

Let us now imagine that there is an elaborated plan for capital investments in the basic branches of the national economy in keeping with the requirements of the interbranch balance and with the above-mentioned basic task in the economic policy. A certain sum of capital investments goes to the given branch. Let us assume that this sum is all that the branch can count on and that the sum must be optimally distributed. It may be that this sum is sufficient to produce the necessary quantity of the product. Because, as a rule, enterprises of the factory type yield the greatest surplus product, in this case preference would be given to them. Another case is possible, however, in which modern forms of production cannot guarantee the necessary output with the given sum of capital investments. In this case, one can use a combination of various technological modes such as to attain the given level of production of the gross product and the greatest surplus product. In addition to solving the basic problem (ensuring the necessary volume of production and growth rates), the use of a combination of various technological modes, including the most labor-intensive of them, permits a considerable increase in employment compared with that which would result solely from the use of factory production. Such is the economic formulation of the task. Clearly, as we begin speaking of the production of commodities that the national economy lacks and that otherwise must be imported, we can compare the effect of capital investments on the production of these commodities against the cost of importing them (naturally, taking into account the shortage of foreign currency and the necessary markup on it under these conditions). Comparison must be made not only of the immediate effect of the capital investments but also of their results throughout the entire planning period.

Let us present this problem schematically

(see Fig. 4). Time $(t = 1, 2, 3 \ldots)$ is laid out along the axis of the abscissa. Along the axis of the ordinate are dimensions of annually required output.

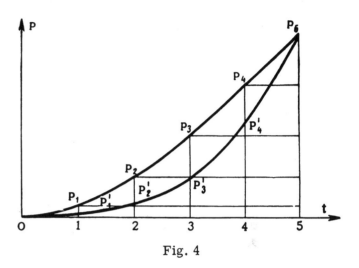

Fig. 4

It is required to use initial capital K in such a way as to maximize the surplus product and simultaneously to guarantee the given dimensions of output P $(P_1, P_2, P_3, \ldots, P_t)$. Points P_1, P_2, $P_3 \ldots$ in the graph depict this target with respect to the dimension of the gross product.

Let us assume that the investment of initial capital K_0 in the "best" mode, i.e., the mode guaranteeing the largest quantity of surplus product, does not serve the attainment of the given level of output (the line P_1', P_2', $P_3' \ldots$). We must therefore choose a combination from n different modes.

Capital invested during the first year is fixed in certain means of production and is operative throughout the entire planning period. During the second year, the capital investments are composed exclusively of accumulations of the first year, i.e., $K_1 = S_1 = m_1$. We find the optimal combination for the second year, etc. If we represent this symbolically, then

$$P_1 = AX;$$

where A = $(a_1, a_2, \ldots, a_n)$ are technological coefficients;

$$X = (X_1, X_2, \ldots, X_n); \quad \sum_{i=1}^{n} X_i = K_0.$$

$$P_2 = P_1 + \Delta P_1 = P_1 + A\Delta_1 X; \quad \Delta_1 = \Delta K_0;$$
$$P_3 = P_2 + \Delta P_2 = P_2 + A\Delta_2 X; \quad \Delta_2 = \Delta(K_0 + \Delta_1);$$
$$\cdots\cdots\cdots\cdots\cdots\cdots\cdots\cdots\cdots$$
$$P_t = P_{t-1} + \Delta P_{t-1} = P_{t-1} + A\Delta_{t-1}X; \quad \Delta_{t-1} = \Delta(K_0 + \Delta_1 + \ldots + \Delta_{t-2}).$$

We find the optimal combination of various modes for the first year by solving a linear programming problem.

Given: n modes of production; K_0 is the initial sum of capital investments; and M is the total sum of surplus product received as a result of using our chosen combination of technological modes.

$$M = m_1 X_1 + m_2 X_2 + \ldots + m_n X_n.$$

Find max M where

$$\sum_{i=1}^{n} a_i X_i \geqslant P,$$
$$\sum X_i = K_0, \quad X_i \geqslant 0, \quad i = 1, \ldots, n.$$

The number of constraints in the given problem can be increased. Thus, it is possible to introduce an additional constraint on employment (or on the wage fund) as well as a number of constraints on resources (e.g., capital under each mode may be realized not fully but only partly in the dimension $g_1 K_0, g_2 K_0, \ldots, g_n K_0$). Correspondingly there will be an increase in the number of modes participating in the combination.

Having found the optimal combination for the first year, we calculate the sum of the possible surplus product. This surplus product (provided that it is entirely capitalized) is equal to capital K_1 which can be invested in the second year. We check to see whether the additionally required amount of product $P_2 - P_1$ can be produced with capital investments in the amount K_1 solely by using only one, "best" mode, and if not, we again search for the optimal combination of modes now for capital K_1. We perform analogous operations for the third, fourth, ..., t-th years. In this way, the distribution of capital permits us to fulfill the target for the production of product P and simultaneously to find, under the given constraints, the optimal variant for the solution of the problem for the maximi-

zation of M.

If in place of a combination of various modes we select one "best" method permitting a maximum increase in the surplus product, as a result, in the t-th year a large overall amount of surplus product will be produced. Over a period of several years, however, it will be necessary to import the deficit part of the product from abroad, thus expending foreign currency. Accordingly, having selected some combination of modes for t years, it is necessary to compare its effect against the effect of using a single "best" mode.

Let us assume that

Δm is the increment in the accumulation fund (the overall sum of surplus product) as a result of using the "best" mode;

$\Delta' m$ is the part of the general accumulation fund that it is necessary to use for the production of a given quantity P during final year t;

$\Delta m - 'm = m$ is the free "surplus" of capital in the final year, obtained as a result of the use of the "best" mode;

$\sum\limits_{i=1}^{n} \Delta m_i$ is the general increment in the accumulation fund as a result of using combinations of various modes;

$\sum\limits_{i=1}^{n} \Delta' m_i$ is the part of the accumulation fund used in the combination of modes for the production of a given amount P during final year t;

$\sum\limits_{i=1}^{n} \Delta m_i - \sum\limits_{i=1}^{n} \Delta m_i = m'$ is the free "surplus" of capital obtained as a result of using a combination of methods.

Let us assume that $m > m'$.

And $m - m' = h$ is the difference in the free surplus of capital accumulation as a result of the use of the "best" method and the combination of methods.

We shall designate the deficit part of the product resulting from the use of a single mode (see Fig. 4, segments $P_1 P_1'$, $P_2 P_2' \ldots$) by $Q_1, Q_2 \ldots Q_n$.

$$Q = \sum_{i=1}^{t} Q_i; \quad Q_i = P_i - P_i',$$

where P is the given quantity of production, and

P′ is production resulting from the use of a single "best" mode.

The cost of importing the deficit part of the product for the period of t years is equal to rQ, where r is the coefficient that takes into account the difference in purchasing power of currencies and is calculated as was shown above.

In order for the use of the combination of modes to be effective from the viewpoint of the economy as a whole, it is necessary that

$$rQ \geqslant h,$$

i.e., that the outlays (including premiums on foreign currency) for acquiring the deficit portion of output in the case of the use solely of the "best" mode of production exceed the difference in the free "surplus" of capital, which forms as a result of using a single mode and a combination of technological modes.

In the process of solving the given problem, it is possible to proceed from depersonalized technological modes to a concrete coordination of one or another link in the production process with the concrete technological mode. This opens up broad opportunities for cooperation between the factory and small-scale and handicraft enterprises, cooperation in which small-scale production will supplement the factory and not compete with it. In this case, the necessity

for ensuring balanced production will dovetail harmoniously with the interests of securing rapid and stable growth rates for the accumulation fund.

As pointed out above, the economic conditions under which the above-analyzed problem can be posed are very typical for most developing countries. There is no need to demonstrate that the very posing and solution of this problem are possible only if there exist a planning principle in the economy and government regulation and control over the distribution of the resources.

Footnotes

1) H. B. Chenery, The Application of Investment Criteria, p. 83.

2) Ibid., p. 88.

3) Ibid., p. 90.

4) A. K. Sen, Choice of Techniques, pp. 70, 72.

5) The question as to the selection of the basic criterion of economic growth as a whole is open to discussion. In the present work, we cannot discuss this at length. The use of the indicated criterion — balanced growth of the economy — seems to us to be justified for the majority of developing countries that have already begun all-round industrial development and that possess sufficient resources for such development.

CHAPTER VI

The Government and Production Forms with a Low Level of Mechanization

The scientific debates on the economic effectiveness of small-scale production are far from ended. It is, however, indisputable that, at present, official opinion in favor of small-scale and cottage industry, and the necessity of supporting and even developing it, predominates in many developing countries, where this problem is relevant (mass unemployment, etc.). In these countries, financial and other economic aid to small-scale production constitutes a part of the economic policy of the state. To be sure, nowhere does small-scale industry have priority in government capital investments. The principal attention is devoted to the factory industry. Nonetheless, in economic development plans, considerable sums are also allocated for the expansion of small-scale production.

The main criterion for directing capital investments into small-scale industry, e.g., in India, is to provide employment. In this sense, the development of small-scale commodity production is regarded as one of the principal tasks of national economic development. In one of its recommendations, the Indian Planning Commission pointed out: "Only when there is greater employment will it be possible to approve the mechanization of consumer goods production." (1) In the industrial development plan proposed by P. Mahalanobis for the period of India's second five-year plan, provision was also made for the expansion of handicraft production not only with the aim of increasing the volume of consumer goods production but also of substantially increasing the scale of employment. (2) Small-scale and household industry was also given a considerable place in the third five-year plan of India.

The draft of the third five-year plan states: "The approach and policy expressed in the second plan with respect to the village and small-scale industry as a progressive and decentralized sector of the economy should not only be continued but also intensified on the basis of the experience obtained during the implementation of the program of the second five-year plan. Full use should be made of the potential of this industry for the solution of problems of unemployment and underemployment in rural and urban regions and for guaranteeing income and work for specific population groups, e.g., the educated unemployed, refugees, persons moved out of slums, persons from special castes and tribes, landless peasants." (3)

The well-known Indian economist A. K. Dasgupta goes still further. In view of the "menacing" situation with respect to unemployment, he wrote, "the problem of providing employment must occupy a leading position among the tasks of the third five-year plan." (4)

The official policy of Pakistan also includes the support of small-scale production as a form of providing higher employment per unit of invested capital. In Pakistan, however, the approach to capital investment in production with a low level of mechanization is somewhat different than in India.

Here, for example, is the way that the problem of "capital intensive-labor intensive production" was regarded in the draft of Pakistan's first five-year plan: "In recent years there has been extensive discussion concerning the relative value, in underdeveloped countries, of investments aimed at the maximum increase in national income through the use of the most up-to-date technological modes, and investments aimed at providing maximum employment through the use of less modern methods.... In an underdeveloped economy that suffers from a shortage of capital, the question of technology is very important; nonetheless one cannot reject investments in capital-intensive production without careful analysis and weighing all pertinent factors." (5) Noted among these factors is indirect employment, which is usually linked to investments in modern capital-intensive forms of production, and also the creation of a fund from profits that can be used to expand employment. Further, a number of production units, in order for their output to compete on the world market, must be put exclusively on a modern footing and use only the newest equipment. An example of this is the jute industry, the bulk of whose output is intended for export.

The draft plan states: "In our recommendations, we emphasize the necessity for developing small-scale and household industry that promises high employment per unit of capital, in those instances when production is relatively effective or can be made effective." (6) The plan warns against excessive fascination both with the most capital-intensive forms of production (automation), considering that in the face of cheap manpower these forms will be completely unprofitable, as well as with extremely backward forms, the use of which, in the opinion of the authors of the plan, will lead to a "decline in the national income growth rates and to an overall reduction in the potential for additional employment." (7)

Pakistan's second five-year plan interprets this approach to small-scale industry in still more specific terms. As the basic goal of industrial policy, the plan advances the "encouragement of those branches and enterprises from which the greatest contribution to the national income per unit of capital investment is anticipated." (8) In other words, in Pakistan the principal criterion for capital investment is considered to be the amount of net output per unit of capital investment. It is declared that small-scale industry, as a means of providing employment, has the right to exist only if it can withstand comparison with factory industry with respect to such an indicator as the "net output-capital" ratio.

Nonetheless, despite possible individual deviations in the approach to small-scale industry in one or another developing country, these governments see an important economic and social problem in the utilization of production forms with a low level of mechanization.

But what are the prerequisites for using small-scale industry in the developing countries?

The Accumulation Fund in Small-Scale Industrial Commodity Production

Two questions arise in this connection: what is the relationship of the necessary and surplus product in the net output of the small-scale industrial commodity production, and what part of small-scale industry's accumulation goes to meet the needs of expanded reproduction in small-scale industry itself? Owing to the sparseness and incompleteness of existing statistical data, our calculations will inevitably be of the most approximate nature.

The official statistics of India contain data on national income, including income created in small-scale industry. By finding the proportion in which this income breaks down into the necessary and surplus product, (9) we obtain absolute figures on the consumption fund and accumulation fund in the small-scale commodity sector. According to our data (see Table 3), this proportion varies from 0.80 (the share of surplus product in net product) in the soap making industry to 0.08 in the metallurgical industry; most frequently it is 30-40%. Other sources give already weighted average indica-

88

tors for basic branches in the small-scale and household industry.

According to the data of the National Sample Survey, (10) the amount of value added per worker in small-scale industry is 32 rupees a month. In a year this amounts to 384 rupees. Outlays on wages constitute 16 rupees a month or 192 rupees a year per worker. Accordingly, the surplus product created by one worker in the course of a year equals: $384 - 192 = 192$ rupees. The relationship m/Y, or the share of the surplus product in the value added here, is 50%.

The average weighted data of the survey on small-scale industry in Moradabad give another picture. Here the average amount of value added is 702 rupees per worker. The wage of the hired worker is 615 rupees. Accordingly, the surplus product is only 87 rupees. The share of the surplus product in the total value added is 12%. Such low dimensions of the net product of Moradabad's small-scale industry are chiefly explained by the fact that among small-scale enterprises the very small enterprises predominate (four or less workers), and in these enterprises the amount of value added is indeed phenomenally low — on the average for all branches, 456 rupees a year per worker. But for the other groups, these indicators are considerably higher: 1,496 rupees for enterprises with 5-9 workers, 1,147 for enterprises with 10-14 workers, and 1,460 for enterprises with 15-19 workers. (11) It is clear that the share of the surplus product in the value added will also be considerably higher for these groups of enterprises (46-59%).

Let us take 12% and 50% as the lowest and highest boundaries of the share of the surplus product in the net product of small-scale industry. In this case, the minimum and maximum volume of the fund of potential accumulation will be as shown in the table (in billions of rupees). (12)

Thus, according to the most modest estimates, India's small-scale industry annually creates a potential accumulation fund in excess of 1 billion rupees. To be sure, as noted above, the wage level here is extremely low even for an

| Years | Net product | Size of surplus product of small-scale industry with its share in the net product of: | |
		12%	50%
1948/49	8.70	1.04	4.35
1950/51	9.10	1.09	4.55
1951/52	8.70	1.04	4.35
1952/53	9.30	1.11	4.65
1953/54	9.80	1.18	4.90
1954/55	10.30	1.24	5.15
1955/56	10.20	1.22	5.10
1956/57	9.80	1.18	4.90
1957/58	9.60	1.15	4.80
1958/59	10.10	1.21	5.05
1959/60	9.50	1.14	4.75

economically underdeveloped country. Nonetheless, this is the actual volume of consumption in small-scale industry. The surplus product remaining after deduction of consumption is, in our opinion, completely realistic. It is precisely from this surplus product that the large army of middlemen operating in the sphere of small-scale commodity production reap their income. The question as to how this potential accumulation fund is used and into what parts it breaks down is another thing. Before turning to this question, we must voice one objection to Indian economist G. Menon, a representative of vulgar bourgeois political economy.

Menon maintains: "...net value (newly created value — S. K.), created by the average worker under given conditions, can be exchanged only for net value created by another average worker working under the same conditions. The household industry uses primitive forms of production, and the value created by each worker is low. Therefore, this value is sufficient only for purchasing a product created by another such worker and not for purchasing factory goods, which are much more expensive. Accordingly, the workers in the household industry form an isolated economy, the products of which to a considerable extent are exchanged within it. Only to the extent that it can sell its output to outsiders (outside consumers) can this economy increase its well-being, and this does not happen in the majority of cases. These circumstances can explain the poverty of workers employed in the household industry and indicate the direction in which steps must be taken to lessen this poverty." (13)

The claim that the small commodity sector is a "closed economy" is not true. Both with respect to raw materials supply and the sale of finished output, the craftsmen are closely linked to a broad market, in particular to the factory industry. For the majority of branches in small-scale industry, these ties are more important than those that small-scale commodity producers have with one another. The latter ties have great significance only for organic manufactures (both organized and dispersed) that represent a productive chain for the manufacturing of a single commodity. The close link between present-day small-scale production and the entire economic complex, and the existence of this production as one of the as yet necessary elements in social reproduction, constitute one of the important features in the economics of developing countries.

But even if one does not take Menon's expression concerning the product that the small-scale commodity sector can sell to "outsiders" and thus "increase its well-being" literally but rather as a concept of a certain "surplus" in "net value" (evidently in excess of the means of subsistence for workers of the household industry), the idea that this "surplus" is an infrequent occurrence and that this explains the poverty of workers employed in small-scale industry is also very disputable.

Undoubtedly, as a rule the surplus product created by the worker in small-scale commodity production is less than that created in the modern factory industry. Nonetheless, this "surplus" does exist and, according to our estimates, on a very considerable scale. And it could not be otherwise, taking into account the sums that the government receives from the small-scale commodity sector in the form of taxes and the above-mentioned incomes of moneylenders and merchants connected with small-scale producers.

Even proceeding a priori from the scope of such a phenomenon as the middleman, we can say that considerable sums representing the surplus product of small-scale industry are concentrated in the hands of the numerous moneylenders and merchants servicing this branch. G. Menon himself points out that "owing to the existence of middlemen, the value received by the producer is much less than that paid by the consumer." (14)

As established above, the minimum dimensions of accumulation in India's small-scale industrial commodity production during 1948/49-1959/60 exceeded 1 billion rupees a year. Total government subsidies and small-scale industry's investments during the first five-year plan (1950-1955) constituted 437 million rupees or approximately 87 million rupees a year. (15) Capital investment in small-scale production from the private sector during the first five-year plan is not known. According to data cited in the book by Coale and Hoover, (16) the volume of net investment (private and government) in the fixed capital of small-scale industry (including the production of agricultural implements) was 600 million rupees for 1953/54. If one takes this figure as an average, the total sum of capital investments for the period 1950/51-1954/55 would be 3 billion rupees. According to our estimates, the minimum sum of small-scale industry's surplus product was 5.66 billion rupees. Thus, the free "surplus" of capital in excess of funds spent on expanding production in small-scale industry itself during the first plan reached a minimum of 2.66 billion rupees.

During the second five-year plan, government outlays for the needs of small-scale industry amounted to 1,800 million rupees or 360 million rupees a year. (17) Private capital investment for the same period was estimated at 2,250 million rupees or 450 million rupees a year. (18) If we take even the very minimal sum of surplus product created during this period in small-scale industry (5.9 billion rupees) and subtract outlays of a capital nature on its own needs, the free "surplus" of capital will amount to 1.85 billion rupees.

It should be noted that the minimal sums of surplus product used by us unquestionably understate the actual sum of the free "surplus" of capital in small-scale industry. The real magnitude of this "surplus" lies between the minimal and maximal points.

Even the most approximate estimates show that small-scale industrial commodity production under the conditions of developing countries has not as yet lost its significance as a potential source of initial capital accumulation. The question as to the degree to which this source is realized is linked to the use of the surplus product that falls into the hands of the middlemen. Unquestionably, a considerable part of this surplus product goes into nonproductive parasitic consumption, while another part is transformed into merchant-moneylender capital (expansion of merchant and moneylender functions, etc.).

In recent years, the merchant, the moneylender, the artisan, and the small entrepreneur more and more willingly invest free capital in the stock of large industrial companies. Thus, small-scale industry, being destroyed and squeezed by large-scale production, creates additional possibilities for the growth and consolidation of the latter.

According to rough estimates cited above, the overall sum of investments in small-scale and cottage industry in India during the first and second five-year plans (1950-1960) amounted to approximately 7 billion rupees. At the same time, the income created in this industry increased very slightly compared with the 1950 base year. What does this fact tell us? In our opinion, we see here a clash between two opposing trends: the attempt to increase small-scale production on the basis of additional government as well as private investment on the one hand, and the continuous displacement of small-scale production by large-scale production on the other.

Convincing material on the continuous process of "erosion" of small-scale and handicraft production in India, and on the continuous disappearance of small enterprises and the emergence of new ones, is cited in the book by Soviet economist N. A. Savel'ev. (19) Government financing

of small-scale industry and the specific features of the economic situation in developing countries — features that induce the private sector as well to be increasingly active in investing in its development — thus serve as one of the factors holding back the disintegration of small-scale production.

For Pakistan the size of the accumulation fund in small-scale industry can only be found by a rather complex route. As initial data, we shall take figures on income in small-scale industry for 1949/50-1962/63. It should be noted that the amount of surplus value created in small-scale industry, as in other spheres of material production, is inevitably somewhat lower in the official statistics of Pakistan because part of it is counted in other, nonmaterial spheres, particularly in trade, bank dealings, services, etc. Unfortunately, there is no way to correct this error. The matter is complicated still further by virtue of the fact that the "surplus value-value added" ratio is very different for the various branches of Pakistan's small-scale industry. In order to find the average ratio for all industry, it is necessary to select the corresponding weights. The share of each branch in the newly created value of small-scale industry (see Table 10) may serve as such weights.

Using these weights and the branch coefficients "surplus value-value added," we find the average weighted ratio equal to

$$\frac{0.53 \cdot 38.1 + 0.51 \cdot 24.0 + 0.28 \cdot 4.9 + 0.23 \cdot 0.8}{100}$$
$$\frac{+ 0.35 \cdot 0.8 + 0.45 \times 0.9 + 0.35 \cdot 30.5}{100} = 0.46.$$

The average ratio obtained refers to 1954. Strictly speaking, in order to find each new average coefficient for preceding and subsequent years, it is necessary to use other weights. Since we do not have such data at our disposal, however, and since it is known that for the selected period the structure of small-scale industry has not undergone significant changes, it seems possible to us to use the coefficient derived above for finding the amount of surplus

Table 10

Pakistan. Share of Basic Branches of Small-Scale Industry in Value Added in 1954*
(millions of rupees)

Branch	Gross product (P)	Value added (y)	"Added gross product" ratio $\left(\frac{y}{P}\right)$	Share in total value added (%)	"Surplus value-value added" ratio
Food	2,612.4	381.8	0.15	38.1	0.53
Textile (cotton)	525.0	241.7	0.46	24.0	0.51
Leather and leather goods (footwear)	130.7	49.7	0.38	4.9	0.28
Glass, ceramics	18.2	7.5	0.41	0.8	0.23
Light chemistry	43.5	7.4	0.17	0.8	0.35
Metal goods	27.7	10.5	0.38	0.9	0.45
Other	767.5	307.0	0.40**	30.5	0.35
Total	4,125.0	1,005.6	–	100.0	–

*The First Five-Year Plan 1955-1960, Government of Pakistan National Planning Board, Karachi, 1958, pp. 482-484. Data on the relationship y/P and also on m/y are calculated on the basis of Table 4.
**For many other branches, such as plastics production and dyeing and printing of textiles, the relationship y/P stays within 0.4-0.5. Therefore, for the "other" column this relationship is conditionally taken as 0.4.

product in small-scale industry for all years of the selected period.

Notwithstanding the considerable size of the potential accumulation fund created in preceding years in small-scale industry (approximately 7.7 billion rupees), the expansion of this industry has been very slow and insignificant. If one judges by data on the size of the income produced, in the space of 14 years, production in Pakistan's small-scale industry has increased by only 40%, which clearly is not in keeping with the possibilities that the accumulation fund created in this branch has presented. The fragmentary data at our disposal permit us to conclude that for all the years of Pakistan's independent existence merchant-moneylender capital has invested in the development of small-scale and handicraft production. A number of branches in small-scale industry were essentially created anew during this period. None-

theless, the reverse trend — the destruction and disappearance of small enterprises under the pressure of large ones, similar to that noted for India — has hindered and weakened the growth of small-scale industrial commodity production. It is also unquestionable that a considerable, if not the greater, part of the surplus product created in Pakistan's small-scale industry has gone to other spheres of the national economy.

The intensive development of industry in the period of Pakistan's independence, (20) the protectionist policy of the government vis-a-vis private capital—in particular, a very favorable tax setup for new industrial construction — all these things helped to bring about a situation whereby a considerable part of the surplus product that had accumulated in the hands of moneylenders and merchants was directed into the industrial entrepreneurial sphere. According to

92

Table 11

Pakistan. Accumulation Fund and Consumption
Fund in Small-Scale Industry*
(constant prices of 1949/50-1952/53;
millions of rupees)

Fiscal year	Net income	Accumu-lation fund	Consump-tion fund
1949/50	1,001	460	541
1950/51	1,017	467	550
1951/52	1,053	483	570
1952/53	1,081	497	584
1953/54	1,109	510	599
1954/55	1,139	524	615
1955/56	1,171	539	632
1956/57	1,202	552	650
1957/58	1,234	567	667
1958/59	1,267	582	685
1959/60	1,302	599	703
1960/61	1,337	614	723
1961/62	1,375	632	743
1962/63	1,411	650	761
Total	16,699	7,676	9,023

*Pakistan Basic Facts, Karachi, 1963, p. 105.

the data of Professor Nurul Islam, Dean of the Department of Economics of Dacca University, during the period 1949-1959, 14% of all capital investments in Pakistan's factory industry were covered by profits from trade. (21) Under the system that dates back to colonial times in countries like India and Pakistan, merchants, even the most powerful merchants, usually carry out their commercial-moneylending activities (through a network of smaller middlemen and agents) among the peasantry and craftworkers. The exploitation of the peasants and the craft workers is one of the sources of industrial capital formation in modern Pakistan. Calculations of the surplus product being formed in small-scale industry give an approximate idea of the size of this source. There was a very intensive flow of merchant-moneylender

capital into commercial and credit operations as well. The smaller incomes of the middlemen settled in the safes of national and foreign banks operating in the nation. During the same period (1949-1962), the total of deposits in the largest commercial banks increased from 1,109 million rupees to 4,562 million rupees, or by more than 4 times. (22)

Yet another circumstance should be considered. In calculating the size of the value added and of surplus value, we have proceeded from the fact that small-scale industry has a fixed capital amortization fund and that the amortization norm in it is just as high as in the factory industry — 10% of the value of the fixed capital. In practice, however, the fixed capital of small-scale industry, particularly of the household crafts, is not amortized for decades; the craftsmen continue to work with tools inherited from previous generations, while those sums that we conditionally classify as amortization fund frequently go to the moneylender or merchant to pay for raw materials, means of subsistence, and rents for work place. Thus the amount of the product appropriated by the middleman stratum is still higher. At the same time, in the matter of improving working conditions and acquiring more productive machinery, even that with a low level of mechanization, small-scale industry itself is dependent on government doles or on infrequent and meager credits from commercial banks.

The merchant-moneylender stratum, exploiting craftsmen and small entrepreneurs, does not strive for any kind of change in the existing situation. "Many small enterprises, particularly in the domestic industry, get along without a mechanical engine and with very few, extremely primitive work tools," the first five-year plan of Pakistan notes. "Small-scale industry encounters difficulties both in securing working capital and in acquiring improved equipment. The banks are seldom disposed to extend credit directly to the small entrepreneurs. Other sources of such credit are absent, and without credit there can be no modernization. (23)

The statistics available on other developing countries do not permit any kind of calculation of the accumulation fund in small-scale industrial commodity production. We can only cite additional data on Burma, showing that the share of the surplus product in the value added of small-scale industry, while smaller than in the factory industry, is nonetheless rather large. Thus, according to the 1953 census, each worker in small-scale industry creates 864 kyat of "value added" a year and receives 420 kyat in the form of wages. If one subtracts the amortization of fixed capital (10% of 286 kyat of fixed capital per worker), the net product is 836 kyat. Accordingly, the average surplus product per worker in Burma's small-scale industry is 416 kyat or about half of the net product. In 1953, the overall sum of the net product of small-scale industry (less fixed capital amortization) was 77 million kyat or about 35% of the total net product created in the manufacturing industry. (24) According to our estimates, the surplus product of Burma's small-scale industry this year will be 38.5 million kyat.

The calculations presented in this section show that the potential of production with a low level of mechanization as a source of capital accumulation for the national economy is still far from exhausted, that this type of production is deserving of the government's closest attention. True, the scattered nature of small-scale production, the lowering of its productive efficiency as a result of poor raw material supply, etc., factory competition, the plunder of capital accumulated in it by numerous middlemen, and other negative factors sharply reduce the value of this source. However, these very same factors also suggest a way for the more effective use of the possibilities hidden in small-scale production: government management of its activities, higher efficiency through more rational organization, and the concentration in government hands of that part of the surplus product that at the present time falls into the hands of the middlemen.

Government Support of Small-Scale Commodity Production. "Industrial Estates"

According to economist K. T. Ramakrishna's classification, the system of government mea-

sures to support India's small-scale industry includes financial and nonfinancial aid. The aid is administered both by the central government and by the governments of states in coordination with the central government. (25)

Small enterprises and cooperatives receive loans from the central budget, from the budgets of states as well as from various government and semigovernment institutions (in particular, from the National Corporation for Small-Scale Industry of India and the Corporation of Small-Scale and Cottage Industry of Pakistan), government banks (the Reserve Bank of India, the State Bank of Pakistan), and others. One can also classify various tax benefits for small-scale industry as financial aid.

Nonfinancial government support to small-scale industry takes the form of technical consultation, the organization of production training, the sale of output, assistance in acquiring raw materials and equipment, etc. One of the most important forms of government aid to small-scale industry in India, which Ramakrishna classifies as nonfinancial aid, is the organization of so-called industrial estates.

However, the practical scale of financial aid to small-scale industry both in India and in Pakistan up to now has been relatively small. Thus, as of December 31, 1957, loans from India's government financial institutions to the small-scale commodity sector amounted to only 22.4 million rupees. As Ramakrishna notes, the granting of a loan to small entrepreneurs is accompanied by a very complex and drawn-out procedure, as a result of which many entrepreneurs are practically bereft of the possibility of getting a loan even if a certain sum has been allocated for this purpose in the government budget. (26) For the period of the second five-year plan (1955/56-1960/61) this sum was increased to 200 million rupees. (27)

Under the first five-year plan of Pakistan, government aid to small-scale production was set in the amount of 86.5 million rupees. The bulk of this money was to go for the acquisition of raw materials, for the purchase and export of commodities, for assistance in the organization of cooperative societies and "industrial

94

estates." (28) The program for the development of small-scale industry during Pakistan's second five-year plan makes provision for larger allocations — 500 million rupees, which must be realized through federal and provincial corporations of small-scale and cottage industry. The bulk of the allocations under the second five-year plan is for the organization of technical servicing, aid in the supply of materials and sales, and extension of credit. (29)

In India, the organization of the sale of small-scale industry's commodities has not acquired any serious dimension. In a number of states, the government has organized the purchase of these commodities for government needs. The Bureau of India Railways has concluded a contract with small entrepreneurs for the delivery of certain types of goods. Nonetheless, all these purchases are as yet insignificant. Official Indian circles look upon them only as a beginning. It is notable that during recent years the National Corporation for Small-Scale Industry of India has constantly been trying to obtain orders for small-scale industry not only from state-owned but also from large privately owned factory enterprises, attempting in this way to exploit the emerging trend to subordinate the crafts and manufactures to large-scale modern production and to make the existence of small-scale industry easier. At the same time, India's government extends certain tax benefits and preferences in prices to small-scale commodity production in order to increase the latter's ability to compete in the struggle with factory production.

Simultaneously with attempts to facilitate the sale of small-scale industry's products on the internal market, the National Corporation for Small-Scale Industry of India (in Pakistan — the Corporation of Small-Scale and Cottage Industry) attempts to have small-scale industry's products sold in external markets. As regards custom-made goods produced by traditional small-scale production, their export is rising steadily even though they do not play any significant role in the nation's total exports. Naturally, the capacity of the internal market for these goods is limited; with the generally favor-

able business conditions, however, the world market for these goods can be considered assured. Much greater difficulties are encountered in selling on foreign markets the output of small enterprises producing consumer goods. Certain of these goods, e.g., Indian footwear, Pakistani sporting goods, already have an assured market abroad. Most of other goods, however, cannot be exported in view of the fact that their quality is below that of the factory industry and they are not standard. As noted in official documents, "Owing to the low quality of Indian commodities (goods produced by small-scale industry — S. K.), they cannot find a market abroad even though in terms of their price they are able to compete." (30) In addition to increasing labor productivity, the system of technical consultations and expert assistance for small-scale production also aims at improving the quality of the output of small-scale production. (31)

In countries like India, great hopes are placed on the organization of cooperative sale of small-scale industry's goods. As Ramakrishna writes, "In the future, cooperative sale should solve the market problems for small-scale industry." (32) At the present time, however, small producers are, as a rule, entirely dependent on a middleman — a merchant or moneylender — in the sale of their goods.

One of the most important government measures vis-à-vis small-scale industry, a measure to which much importance is attached, is the sale of equipment on credit. The down payment is 20% of the cost of the equipment and the remaining sum is paid off over a seven-year period at the rate of 6% a year (from 1956 to 1959). In India, during four years of the operation of the system for selling equipment on credit, 3,000 machine tools for a total of 26 million rupees were sold to small-scale industry. (33) If the equipment is acquired abroad, the National Corporation for Small-Scale Industry of India must supply the small entrepreneurs with the necessary foreign currency. In this connection, the need for foreign currency on the part of the National Corporation for Small-Scale Industry of India is assessed at 13 million rupees a year. (34) The program for the sale of equipment on credit has also been adopted in Pakistan. (35) As we know, however, both countries — India and Pakistan — are experiencing an acute shortage of foreign currency for more pressing needs. There is frequently, therefore, a large gap between the requests by small-scale industry for foreign currency and that which the corporations can actually grant.

The program to aid small-scale industry, adopted in India and Pakistan, including the extension of hard-to-get foreign currency to it, aims at "correcting the situation" with its low fixed capital per worker and at gradually "modernizing" it to the level of the factory industry. (36) Like other measures by the governments of India and Pakistan, these programs are as yet in the nature of plans for the future. Nonetheless, in the second five-year plan of Pakistan, provision is already made for the allocation of considerable sums for the technical outfitting and modernization of small enterprises.

In view of difficulties with foreign currency for the purchase of modern equipment, the government of India is selling small entrepreneurs obsolete equipment that cannot be used in the factory industry. (37) Because the factory industry itself has for a long time been selling obsolete equipment to small-scale industry, this measure by the National Corporation for Small-Scale Industry in India is nothing but an attempt to bring this widespread practice into a planned channel and to some extent to place it under the control of the government.

Particular mention should be made of the economic content of such a form of government support of small-scale production as the organization of "industrial estates." As Indian economist S. V. Kapade observes, "The creation of industrial estates as a means of stimulating small and medium-size enterprises throughout the entire country is at the present time the common feature of our programs and policy for the development of industry." (38)

The "industrial estate" is a plot of land upon which industrial and residential buildings are erected. These are supplied with water mains, electricity, and communications. Unlike

the developed capitalist countries, where the construction of "industrial estates" was chiefly done by private capital, sometimes with government aid, in India, Pakistan, and other developing nations the construction of "industrial estates" is carried out chiefly by the government. The degree of equipment of "industrial estates" up to the point where they are taken over by the first entrepreneurs may differ. Some "estates" are only given a building site and such items necessary for production as water, electricity, and communications, while others are given production buildings and sometimes housing as well, on a lease or credit basis. In India it is precisely such "completely outfitted industrial estates" that predominate, while in Pakistan the creation of "industrial estates" includes the preparation of the production area and the basic amenities for general use. (39)

In India, the program for the construction of "industrial estates" has been in operation since 1955. By mid-1960, the construction of 120 "estates" was sanctioned, of which 40 had already been completed by that time. The latter should place 1,343 small enterprises employing approximately 15,000 persons. Not only do the small entrepreneurs on these "estates" receive production buildings and general conveniences; they also receive technical-economic consultations, certain benefits with respect to loans for the purchase of stocks and equipment, etc. During the third five-year plan it is intended to increase the total number of "industrial estates" in India to 380. The estimated cost of construction at all "estates" is approximately 500 million rupees. (40)

In Pakistan, two large "industrial estates" (both in Western Pakistan) have gone into operation. During the second five-year plan it is intended to construct 24 "industrial estates" in both parts of the country with an overall projected cost of 36 million rupees. (41)

It is characteristic that even though up to now both in India and in Pakistan the "industrial estates" have been created exclusively in the government sector, beginning with 1960 there has been a tendency for private capital to penetrate this area. As noted in an official UN publication, in India "in 1960, owing to the growing demand for industrial estates in many regions of the country the government has decided to stimulate the development of industrial estates by means of private capital." (42)

In 1961, the construction of "industrial estates" by private capital was sanctioned by a special act. For its part, the government guaranteed its material support and a number of benefits for this construction. Thus, under the act on "private industrial estates," operative in Rajasthan, a company undertaking the construction of an "estate" is rented a plot of land, water and electrical facilities are set up, a bank loan is guaranteed, etc. (43)

A similar picture is observed in Pakistan. In December 1961, it was proposed to the government of Eastern Pakistan that the rights of the Corporation for Small-Scale and Cottage Industry be expanded and that it be given the right to build enterprises in conjunction with private firms, cooperative societies, and private persons. It was supposed that in the future the corporation could transfer certain units, including "industrial estates," from the government to the private sector. (44)

The growing trend in these countries to transfer "industrial estates" to the private sector can be explained by two basic reasons. The first of these is the financial difficulties of the governments of India and Pakistan, which hinder not only the expansion of the construction of "industrial estates" but also the fulfillment of already outlined industrial programs. Second, private capital in these countries has itself become interested in the "industrial estates" and in the possibility of a broader and, if it can be expressed this way, a more organized exploitation of small-scale production.

Even now there are certain facts that indicate that private capital in India is striving to take the organization of "industrial estates" into its own hands. For example, W. Bredo, an American student of small-scale industry in India, reports the following facts. After an "industrial estate" in Rajkot had been built along government lines, the government of the state of Gujarat received simultaneously three proposals

to build "industrial estates" in the given region: from a private person, from a group of industrialists, and from the municipality of the city of Rajkot. (45)

What is the meaning of the "industrial estates"? We find the answer to this question in a statement of the Indian government concerning its industrial policy. "Industrial estates" are faced with the goals: (1) of accelerating the development of small-scale production; (2) of providing conditions favoring the attainment and maintenance of a high level of productivity of the enterprises located on the "estates"; and (3) of promoting the creation of a system of inter-branch relationships and complementarity among various branches of industry. (46)

It is still too early to judge the extent to which the first and third points of this program will be fulfilled; there is still too little experience with "industrial estates." As to the second point, it is already possible to draw certain conclusions even though materials on this question are very scant. Unfortunately, these conclusions are not in favor of the "industrial estates" (see Table 12).

The data for the "estate" in Ludhiana are comparatively low owing to difficulties with respect to business conditions. Nonetheless, the very low "net output-capital" ratio in the "industrial estates" is evident. In other "estates" the situation is even less favorable. (47)

As can be seen in Table 12, the "net output-capital" ratio at enterprises of the "industrial estates" is much lower than the corresponding ratio in scattered small-scale industry (compare with Table 3). The lowest boundary of the given ratio in dispersed small-scale industry is 0.60 (chemical and pharmaceutical industry). In the majority of cases, the indicators for factory industry are also higher than the "net output-capital" ratio observed at enterprises of the "industrial estates." Only the data for the "estate" in Okkhla somewhat approach the level of the factory industry. Thus, as the data show, there is no "saving of capital" on the "industrial estates." All this gives Dhar and Lydall the grounds for saying that "purely from the point of view of economizing on capital it is difficult

India. Economic Indicators of Enterprises Joined into "Industrial Estates"*
(rupees)

Estate	Average number employed at enterprise	Value added per unit of capital	Value added per worker	Amount of capital per worker
Okkhla	46	0.41	2,535	6,341
Ludhiana	9	9.21	1,973	7,807
Sanatnagar	21	0.27	3,199	12,479
State of Kerala	17	0.15	1,069	5,074
Average for all estates	19	0.31	2,037	6,992

*P.N. Dhar and H.F. Lydall, The Role of Small Enterprises in Indian Economic Development, p. 54.

to justify the construction of industrial estates." (48)

At the same time, the available capital per worker on the "industrial estates" is much higher than capital per worker in dispersed small-scale industry. The lowest level of capital per worker on the "industrial estates" is 5,074 rupees, while in dispersed small-scale industry it is 2,940 rupees (see Tables 12 and 3). In terms of amount, the capital per worker in the "industrial estates" is only a little less and for certain branches even exceeds the level that is predominant in the factory industry. Even though the amount of value added per worker in the "industrial estates" is higher in a number of instances than in dispersed small-scale industry, the high amount of capital per worker nullifies this advantage. However, the "industrial estates" were conceived precisely as one of the forms of industrial development in the face of a shortage of productive capital. At the same time, the amount of value added per worker on these estates is far from reaching the level of the factory industry (only the indicators for the "estate" in Sanatnagar approach the level of certain branches of the factory industry). Thus, notwithstanding a sharp increase in the capital-output ratio of small-scale commodity production on the "industrial

estates," it has in fact not been possible to achieve a level of labor productivity distinguishing factory industry.

But wherein lies the reason for the low economic effectiveness of the "industrial estates"? Dhar and Lydall see these reasons in the following:

First, in the extremely high cost of building "industrial estates," in the high share of the cost of the land, production buildings, and other overhead expenses of a long-term nature in the value of the fixed capital. According to data cited by them, these elements account for approximately one-half of the total productive capital.

Second, in the fact that the majority of small enterprises on the "industrial estates" for various reasons work a single shift while factory enterprises for the most part work two and even three shifts. Out of the 206 enterprises studied, only 25 worked two shifts on the "industrial estates." (49) Accordingly, the fixed capital on "industrial estates" is underutilized. Dhar and Lydall explain this by citing the inadequate managerial abilities of the small entrepreneurs and their unwillingness to hire managers.

It seems to us that K. T. Ramakrishna comes closer to the truth. He names several causes underlying the failures and difficulties experienced by "industrial estates" in India. Among these are the shortage of raw materials, particularly metal and coke, inadequate technical assistance from the government (technical consultation and training), high rents, and the uneconomical size of the production buildings that are erected. (50)

Thus, frequently the small entrepreneurs themselves are not guilty of underutilizing the equipment. More weighty reasons for this are found in the meagerness of the means at their disposal and also in the shortage of the basic types of raw materials, from which small-scale industry particularly suffers. However, it would be incorrect to stop here.

Even if one substracts the disproportionately large outlays for land and production buildings from the sum of all productive capital of enterprises employed in the "industrial estates," the remaining sum will considerably exceed the value of productive capital in the dispersed small-scale industry. Production on "industrial estates" has a higher capital-output ratio than conventional, small enterprises.

Without question, in this case we are dealing with a particular kind of "overcapitalization," in which small-scale production loses its features as production with a low level of mechanization and the few advantages connected with this, and at the same time does not "reach" the level of the factory industry either in terms of the organic composition of capital or the level of labor productivity.

The "overcapitalization" of small-scale industry on the "industrial estates" is not accidental. This is a manifestation of a policy for "modernizing" existing small enterprises. W. Bredo observes: "In Puerto Rico and India industrial estates are used as a means of stimulating entrepreneurship, of creating new industry and, in the case of India, of modernizing existing enterprises." (51)

Clearly, the enterprises "being modernized" cannot endlessly remain in such an indeterminate position, a position in which they in fact are already separated from small-scale industry as industry with a low level of mechaniza-

tion; at the same time they have not become factory enterprises in the modern sense of the word. As can be seen from the above data, it will be unprofitable for the national economy to keep them in this state. In this case, "industrial estates" will be simply a costly experiment and will not make that contribution to the economic development of the country that is expected of them.

Yet it is our deep conviction that "industrial estates" can, after certain adjustments, become one of the important tools of government support and regulation of industrial development. Two possible roads of development of "industrial estates" are conceivable.

One road is the further increase in their capital-output ratio, with the ultimate goal of creating a modern factory industry with its "extravagance" with respect to capital but with a greater labor productivity than in other forms of industrial production.

The second road is to develop "industrial estates" as a form of "organized" small-scale production and to use to the limit (during the transitional period in the development of the economy) the ability of this production to guarantee, in a short space of time, e.g., 10-15 years, a greater gross and net product for the same capital than would exist in the factory industry.

From the economic point of view, the first road would mean the growth of modern industry out of the lower forms of production rather than the use of industry with a low level of mechanization in the interests of satisfying today's needs of the national economy. Clearly, before pursuing this goal it should be decided whether it would be more economically advisable directly to create modern forms of industry than to try to reach this goal by "modernizing" backward forms.

From the social point of view, the first road, in our opinion, conceals one serious danger. Under present conditions, the private sector will unquestionably try to use government support for small-scale industry, including such a form as "industrial estates," to stimulate the development of capitalism in the country and to strengthen the private sector. Indicative in this respect is the opinion of the aforementioned economists Dhar and Lydall concerning the road of development of "industrial estates."

"Enterprises on estates use modern and highly mechanized equipment" they write. "These enterprises are not labor-intensive and do not economize on capital and therefore they cannot create great possibilities for employment as compared with average and large factories producing the same commodity. The meaning of industrial estates is rather that they serve as a cradle that can promote the growth of capable small entrepreneurs. If this goal were more firmly adhered to, there would be fewer vain attempts to grow 'new' entrepreneurs and the costly new utilities would not be given to people who do not know how to make proper use of them." (52)

In another passage, the authors are even more specific: "Industrial estates should be viewed not as a haven for the weak and inept but as the cradle of small entrepreneurship. It should be recognized that many firms settled on the industrial estates will grow so that in time they will become too big for the estate. Accordingly, it would be desirable to provide firms that have distinguished themselves with conditions whereby they could build their own factories in nearby regions with the proper financial support." (53)

The position of Dhar and Lydall differs in no way from the positions of other proponents of the capitalist road of development. The only difference is that the aforementioned authors favor the creation of a class of "middle capitalists." However, capitalism (private initiative) with every passing day increasingly demonstrates its inability to solve the problem of the accelerated development of the material level of economically underdeveloped countries. Therefore the wish of certain circles in the developing countries to subject the government completely to the interests of the private sector at every step contradicts the actual needs of the national economy of these countries.

The program for modernizing existing small enterprises may prove to be very useful, however, only in those places where it promises faster and cheaper creation of additional capacities than does new construction. Under the conditions in which the presently developing countries find themselves, in a number of cases the second road of development of "industrial estates" may prove more expedient.

As shown above, the overhead expenses in "dispersed" small-scale industry are very great. Even though at the present time these overhead expenses are still higher on the "industrial estates," nonetheless with more rational organization "industrial estates" could become precisely the means for lowering overhead expenses in small-scale production and on such a scale that it would be difficult for "dispersed" small-scale industry to attain. The decrease in capital outlays will considerably increase the profitability of this form of industrial production. In order to attain this goal it is necessary from the very beginning to view "industrial estates" as a form of organization of production with a low level of mechanization and not as an incubator of "small" capitalists.

It is possible that the further development of "industrial estates" will lead to the transition of these to a higher form — producers' cooperatives. This will immediately make possible a sharp reduction in the cost of production buildings and warehouse premises, utilities (gas, water, electricity), equipment, and production buildings per worker. Producers' cooperatives, in turn, can develop in a direction from common production premises and a common organization of sales to the common possession of the basic means of production. The producers' cooperatives promise the most advantageous organization of small-scale production from the point of view of the entire national economy.

Footnotes

1) S. K. Basu, Place and Problems of Small Industries, p. 81.
2) Ibid., p. 80.
3) Approach to the Third Five-Year Plan: Some Basic Considerations, New Delhi, 1959, p. 5.
4) A. K. Dasgupta, "Understanding 'Take-off,'"

100

AICC Economic Review, Vol. XI, No. 16-18, January 16, 1960, p. 30.

5) The First Five-Year Plan 1955-1960, Vol. 2, Karachi, 1958, p. 227.

6) Ibid.

7) Ibid. This idea has also been repeatedly emphasized in statements by official persons in Pakistan (M. A. Khaleque, "Automation and Labour Problem of Pakistan," Pakistan Economist No. 12-13, June 25-July 10, 1957, p. 10).

8) The Second Five-Year Plan (1960-1965), Karachi, 1960, p. 222.

9) The concept "surplus product" that we are using here is very conditional. The point is that in the small-scale and cottage industry, the necessary product is taken to mean the actual wage of a worker, which is much lower than that of the worker in the factory industry and in a number of cases is even lower than the general living minimum for the nation. Thus, in this case the surplus product inevitably includes a considerable part of the necessary product. It can be called surplus only insofar as it is not part of the actual consumption fund of the small-scale and cottage industry itself.

10) "The National Sample Survey," No. 19, Report on Small-Scale Manufacture, pp. 29-32.

11) Baljit Singh, The Economics of Small-Scale Industries, pp. 37, 63, 56.

12) Papers on National Income and Allied Topics, Vol. 2, Bombay, 1962, p. 33; A. Rudre, "Growth of Income and Output in India, 1948/49-1958/59." Perspective, No. 2, June 1961; P. D. Shirmali, "Small-Scale Cottage and Village Industries," AICC Economic Review, Vol. 14, No. 10, October 7, 1962, p. 18.

By the accumulated part of the net product is meant the entire surplus product, abstracting from nonproductive consumption of part of the surplus product.

13) G. R. B. Menon, Value Economics, Calcutta-New Delhi, 1960, p. 59.

14) Ibid., p. 60.

15) AICC Economic Review, Vol. 14, No. 10, October 7, 1962, p. 17.

16) A. J. Coale and Edgar M. Hoover, Population Growth and Economic Development in Low-Income Countries, Princeton, 1958, p. 150.

17) AICC Economic Review, Vol. 14, No. 10, October 10, 1962, page 17.

18) Taxation and Private Investment, National Council of Applied Economic Research, New Delhi, 1960, p. 24.

19) See N. A. Savel'ev, Melkoe proizvodstvov Indii, Moscow, 1964.

20) The production of the net product in the factory industry of Pakistan increased more than 7 times in the period from 1949/1950 to 1962/63 (Pakistan Basic Facts, 1963, p. 105).

21) Nurul Islam, "Private and Public Enterprises in the Economic Development of Pakistan," Asian Survey, Berkeley (California), Vol. 3, No. 7, July 1963, p. 334.

22) Ibid., p. 87.

23) The First Five-Year Plan 1955-1960, Karachi, 1958, p. 471.

24) Union of Burma, First Stage Census 1953, Vol. 2, pp. 30, 51-60.

25) K. T. Ramakrishna, Finances for Small-Scale Industry in India, pp. 13-16.

26) Ibid., pp. 14, 67.

27) W. Bredo, Industrial Estates. Tool for Industrialization, Bombay, 1962, p. 30.

28) The First Five-Year Plan 1955-1960, p. 479.

29) The Second Five-Year Plan (1960-1965), Karachi, 1960, p. 258.

30) Seminar on Financing of Small-Scale Industries in India, July 1959; K. T. Ramakrishna, Finances for Small-Scale Industry in India, p. 20.

31) Ramakrishna, loc. cit.

32) Ibid., p. 19.

33) P. N. Dhar and H. F. Lydall, The Role of Small Enterprises in Indian Economic Development, p. 72.

34) Ramakrishna, op. cit., p. 22.

35) The Pakistan Times, January 14, 1960.

36) Ibid., March 20, 1960.

37) Ramakrishna, op. cit., pp. 22-23.

38) S. V. Kapade, "Development of Industrial Estates in Rajasthan," The Banker, Delhi, Vol. 9, No. 5, July 1965, p. 282.

39) Bredo, op. cit., p. 3.

40) Ibid., p. 37; United Nations, Establishment of Industrial Estates in Underdeveloped Countries, New York, 1961, pp. 2, 18.

41) Pakistan 1961-1962, Karachi, 1962, p. 43.

42) UN, op. cit., p. 18.

43) P. M. Bhandari, A Guide to Small-Scale Industries, Delhi, 1962, pp. 82-83.

44) The Pakistan Times, December 29, 1961.

45) Bredo, op. cit., p. 65.

46) UN, op. cit., p. 17.

47) Dhar and Lydall, op. cit., p. 55.

48) Ibid.

49) Ibid., pp. 55-56.

50) Ramakrishna, op. cit., p. 27.

51) Bredo, op. cit., p. 8.

52) Dhar and Lydall, op. cit., p. 62.

53) Ibid., p. 87.

Conclusion

Thus, the statistical materials examined above show that in many developing countries, particularly in Asia, there are great possibilities for the use of forms of industrial production having a low level of mechanization. In one or another concrete economic situation very successful use can be made of the positive side of small-scale industry — the greater gross and net output per unit of capital investment as compared with the factory industry. At the same time it should be remembered that large-scale factory production, first of all the production of the means of production, must remain the basis for the industrial development of the countries investigated. Only the development of modern forms of industry can guarantee these countries the most rapid and steady movement along the road of progress. In our view, the present role of small-scale industry is that it makes it possible not to hurry with the development of certain branches and enterprises, i.e., small-scale industry can supply the basic branches with auxiliary output during the entire period of transition to a developed economy. In addition to the fact that such "auxiliary" use of forms with a low level of mechanization will ensure the production of a number of deficit products, it will also considerably increase general employment, and, accordingly, the size of national income. In these forms of production there will be a continuous growth of technical cadres familiar with the principles of a given production unit, able to use at least the most elementary work tools, and possessing certain work skills.

In our opinion, the most promising form for the development of small-scale industry is its organic cooperation with the factory within the framework of the government sector. The development of one or another production facility should be envisaged precisely as a complex in which the leading role belongs to modern industry, while industry with a low level of mechanization takes care of individual links in the production process: manufacture of separate parts, preparation of raw materials, and finishing the final product. Such cooperation between highly mechanized forms of production and forms with a low level of mechanization will make it possible to combine the interests and needs of social reproduction at a given moment and under given conditions with the demands for a maximum increase in the surplus product and thus in the growth rate of a branch as a whole.

Present-day small-scale production in the developing countries requires serious reorganization. Its dispersed nature, the poor organization of sales and supply of raw materials, and the dependence of craft and manufacture on a large number of middlemen sharply reduce the economic effectiveness of small-scale production. It is also necessary to consider the more and more persistent demands to improve the socio-economic situation of the small commodity producers and to liberate them from severe dependence on merchants and moneylenders. Even though under present conditions the craftsman cannot always have the same level of consumption as the factory worker, the elimination of usurious indebtedness and large losses as a result of the commercial "operations" of the middleman can significantly improve the position of the small producer.

Private capital is not interested in such improvements in the economic lot of the craftsmen. On the contrary, the worse situation the latter are in, the more easily can this capital subordinate them. In these countries at the present time, private industrial capital is attempting to put production with a low level of mechanization in its service. However, this frequently forcible symbiosis of factory and small industry may prove ineffective for the national economy as a whole if this matter is placed in the hands of private capital. The capitalist entrepreneur cares little for the needs of the entire branch, for the requirements of the nation for one or another product, and for providing stable interbranch relationships that are most advantageous for the economy as a whole. Naturally, he is first interested in such indicators as the profit norm, the possibility of exploiting the worker by lowering his wages still further and by engaging in various usurious operations, and he is also interested in expanding the range of very small enterprises that consume the output of his enterprise. Only the government can bring about a radical reorganization of small-scale production and guide its further development, observing the interests of society as a whole as well as of the small commodity producers themselves.

The liberation of the craftsman and the small entrepreneur from the "guardianship" of merchants and moneylenders will not only make their existence easier but will also give a great impetus to the expansion and improvement of the production process itself in handicraft and manufacture. Extensive government support of small-scale production, and aid to it in the organization of sales and supply of raw materials, will help the government to control more completely than at the present time the accumulation fund being formed in the small commodity industrial sector.

One of the most promising forms of government support to small-scale and handicraft production is, in our opinion, the organization of the "industrial estates." One can foresee the development of "industrial estates" as industrial complexes combining modern factory and small-scale production. Unquestionably, the further development and improvement of "industrial estates" promises an increase in the effectiveness of small-scale production itself as a result of decreasing production costs and overhead expenses of a capital nature, as well as a greater degree of organization and cooperation in the acquisition of raw materials and in the sale of the finished goods. On the social plane, this measure means support for the entire stratum of the urban petty bourgeoisie against large-scale private capital and monopoly capital under the conditions in India and certain other countries.

The organization of "industrial estates" under government control will expand the sphere of operation of the government sector and, accordingly, its planning base. Moreover, the "industrial estates," if they are organized on a wide enough scale, can become one of the most important tools of the government in planning economic development and in balancing various branches of the national economy. This will also make it possible for the government to exert a more active influence on the entire presently dispersed small-scale commodity sector.

What are the further prospects for the development of the "industrial estates" themselves? Naturally, in large measure this depends on the direction of further development in one or another country. If the ruling circles of some developing country place all their economic resources in the service of the private sector, then the "industrial estates" may indeed become a "cradle for fostering capitalists." But if under the influence of democratic circles in these countries the planning principle will develop more and more and the government sector will grow and strengthen, then the "industrial estates," as already indicated, may become a means of resolving the most important problems of economic development. In this case, the very logic of development will lead small producers to the notion of the necessity for cooperation. Supply-and-sales, and subsequently production cooperation as well, will make it possible to eliminate many of the shortcomings of small-scale production, to increase considerably its profitableness both for the government and for the commodity producers themselves.

Unquestionably, practice may suggest other more flexible forms for using production with a low level of mechanization in developing countries than the "industrial estates." No matter what these forms are, however, only their planned development in connection with other types of production and government support can change them into an important additional reserve for the economic growth of developing countries.

Bibliography

1. Marx, K., Kapital in K. Marx and F. Engels, Soch., Vols. 23-25, Parts 1 and 2.

2. ____, Teorii pribavochnoi stoimosti, op. cit., Vol. 26, Parts 1-3.

3. Lenin, V. I., Razvitie kapitalizma v Rossii, in Poln. sobr. soch., Vol. 3.

4. ____, "Agrarnyi vopros i 'kritiki Marksa,'" op. cit., Vol. 5.

5. ____, "Po povodu tak nazyvaemogo voprosa o rynkakh," op. cit., Vol. 1.

6. ____, "K kharakteristike ekonomicheskogo romatizma," op. cit., Vol. 2.

7. ____, "Kustarnaia perepis' 1894/95 goda v Permskoi gubernii i obshchie voprosy 'kustarnoi' promyshlennosti," op. cit., Vol. 2.

* * *

8. Gorodskie srednie sloi sovremennogo kapitalisticheskogo obshchestva, Moscow, 1963.

9. Kotovskii, G. G., "Ruchnoe promyshlennoe proizvodstvo i rassloenie krest'ianstva na iuge Indii (Tamilnad i Kerala)," Kratkie soobshcheniia Instituta vostokovedeniia, No. XV, Moscow, 1955.

10. Levkovskii, A. I., "O nizshikh formakh kapitalisticheskogo predprinimatel'stva v promyshlennosti Indii (Na primere ruchnogo tkachestva)," Kratkie soobshcheniia Instituta vostokovedeniia, No. XV.

11. ____, Osobennosti razvitiia kapitalizma v Indii, Moscow, 1963.

12. Razvitie promyshlennosti nezavisimoi Indii, Moscow, 1964.

13. Reisner, L. I., "Polozhenie i osnovnye formy melkoi promyshlennosti soedinennykh provintsii Indii v 30-kh godakh XX veka," Kratkie soobshcheniia Instituta vostokovedeniia, No. XXIII, Moscow, 1957.

14. Savel'ev, N. A., Melkoe proizvodstvo v Indii, Moscow, 1964.

15. Fridman, L. A., Kapitalisticheskoe razvitie Egipta, Moscow, 1963.

16. Piganiol', P., "Kriterii pri vybore tekhniki, prednaznachennoi dlia vnedreniia v razvivaiushchikhsia stranakh," United Nations Conference on the Application of Scientific and Technical Knowledge to Satisfy the Needs of the Less Developed Areas, October 19, 1962.

17. "Politika v oblasti zaniatosti s osobym uporom na problemy zaniatosti v razvivaiushchikhsia stranakh," International Labor Conference, Report VIII (I), Geneva, 1963.

18. A Statistical Analysis of Small-Scale Units of the Surgical Instruments Industry, New Delhi, 1962.

19. "Census of Manufacturing Industries, 1957," Statistical Bulletin, Karachi, Vol. 7, No. 12, December 1959.

20. "Census of Small-Scale Manufacturing Industries in Karachi, 1958," Statistical Bulletin, Karachi, Vol. 8, No. 2, February 1960.

106

21. Economic Survey for Asia and the Far East, Bangkok, 1961.

22. Facilities for Small Industries, New Delhi, 1961.

23. "Growth Models for Illustrating the Effects of Alternative Employment and Investment Policies," Economic Bulletin for Asia and the Far East, Bangkok, Vol. 9, No. 1, June 1958.

24. ILO Report to the Government of Indonesia on Labour Statistics, Geneva, 1962.

25. Industry and Mines Statistical Yearbook 1958-1959, Teheran, 1959.

26. Model Schemes on Small-Scale Industries, Vol 1, No. 2. Allahabad, 1960.

27. "Report on the Census of Weaving Industry in Maharashtra State," Quarterly Bulletin of Economics and Statistics, Bombay, Vol. 1, No. 2, July-September 1960.

28. "Scheduled Banks' Advances to Small-Scale Industries and Cooperative Institutions (1960-1961)," Reserve Bank of India Bulletin, Bombay, Vol. 16, No. 11, 1962.

29. "Schemes for Intensive Development of Small Industries in Rural Areas," Indian Information, Delhi, Vol. 5, No. 14, August 15, 1962.

30. Seminar on Financing of Small-Scale Industries in India, Bombay, Vol. 1, No. 2, July 20-23, 1959.

31. Seminar on Industrial Estates in the ECAFE Region. Industrialization and Productivity, New York, No. 5, 1962.

32. Social Aspects of Small Industries in India. Studies in Howrah and Bombay, UNESCO Research Center on Social and Economic Development in Southern Asia, Delhi, 1962.

33. Small-Scale Industries — Procedures and Facilities, New Delhi, 1960.

34. Small-Scale Industries (Programme and Progress), New Delhi, 1959.

35. The All-India Handloom Board Fourth Report 1956-1959, Rajkot, 1959.

36. "The Development of Small-Scale Engineering Industries in Punjab (India)," International Labour Review, Geneva, Vol. 85, No. 6, June 1962.

37. The Indian Cotton Textile Industry (1961 Annual), Bombay, 1962.

38. The National Sample Survey, No. 15, Report on the Sample Survey of Manufacturing Industries, 1951, Delhi, 1958.

39. The National Sample Survey, No. 19. Report on Small-Scale Manufacture, Delhi, 1959.

40. The National Small Industries Corporation, Ltd. Administration Report, New Delhi, 1959.

41. Thirteenth Census of Indian Manufactures 1958, Calcutta, 1961.

42. UN ECA, Economic and Social Council. Draft Programme of Work and Priorities for 1965-1966, E/CN, 14/313, January 28, 1965.

43. UN ECA, Economic and Social Council. Report on Activities in Industry, E/CN, 14/298, November 12, 1964.

44. UN ECA, Economic and Social Council. Outlines and Selected Indicators of African Development Plans, E/CN, 14/336, January 14, 1965.

45. UN ECA, Industrial Growth in Africa. A Survey and Outlook, E/CN, 14/INR/1, December 1962.

46. UN ECA, Report of the ECA Industrial Co-Operation Mission to East and Central Africa, E/CN, 14/247, December 1963.

47. UN, Establishment of Industrial Estates in Underdeveloped Countries, New York, 1961.

48. UN, The Physical Planning of Industrial Estates, New York, 1962.

49. Union of Burma, First State Census 1953, Vol. II, Industry, Cottage Industry and Home Consumed Production Industry, Rangoon, 1958.

* * *

50. Athreya, N. H., "Problems of Growing Business," Commerce and Industry, New Delhi, Vol. 56, No. 2, July 12, 1961.

51. "A New Orientation to Small Industries Development," Journal of Industry and Trade, New Delhi, Vol. 12, No. 6, 1962.

52. Balakrishnan, G., Financing Small-Scale Industries in India, 1950-1952, Poona, 1961.

53. Balakrishnan, R., Review of Economic Growth in India, Bangalore, 1961.

54. Bari, R. K., "The Case of Cottage Industries," Modern Review, Calcutta, Vol. 112, No. 5, November 1962.

55. Basu, S., "Capital-Output-Employment Relationship," AICC Economic Review, New Delhi, Vol. 12, No. 9, September 22, 1960.

56. ___, "Follow-up of Prof. Mahalanobis' Four Sector Model," AICC Economic Review, Vol. 11, No. 16-18, January 16, 1960.

57. ___, "Labour Productivity in Some Indian Industries," AICC Economic Review, Vol. 13, No. 6, August 7, 1961.

58. Basu, S. K., Place and Problems of Small Industries, Calcutta, 1957.

59. Bessaignet, P., Social Aspects of Small Industries, the UNESCO Center's Research Programme, "Yojana," New Delhi, Vol. 6, No. 15, August 5, 1962.

60. Bhalla, A. S., "Galenson-Leibenstein Criterion of Growth Reconsidered. Some Implicit Assumptions," Economia International, Geneva, Vol. 17, No. 2, 1964.

61. Bhandari, P. M., A Guide to Small-Scale Industries, Delhi, 1962.

62. Bhatt, V. V., Employment and Capital Formation in Underdeveloped Economics, Bombay, 1960.

63. Bredo, W., Industrial Estates. Tool for Industrialization, Bombay, 1962.

64. ___, "The Industrial Estate: Social Technology for Economic Development," UN, Conference on the Application of Science and Technology for the Benefit of the Less Developed Areas, November 9, 1962.

65. "Capital Intensity in Industry in Underdeveloped Countries," Industrialization and Productivity, New York, No. 1, 1958.

66. Chenery, H. B., "The Application of Investment Criteria," The Quarterly Journal of Economics," February 1953.

67. Deshpande, M. A., "Small Enterprises: Their Contribution to National Income," Economic Weekly, Bombay, Vol. 14, No. 42, October 1962.

68. Dhar, P. N., Small-Scale Industries in Delhi, Bombay, 1958.

69. ___, and Lydall, H. F., The Role of Small Enterprises in Indian Economic Development, Bombay, 1961.

70. ___, and Sivasubramanian, S., "Small Enterprises," Economic Weekly, Bombay, Vol. 14, No. 28-30, July 1962.

71. Dobb, M., "Planning and Choice of Technique," Perspective, Calcutta, No. 2, June 1961.

72. Dobrska, Z., "The Choice of Techniques in Developing Countries," Center of Research on Underdeveloped Economies, Research Papers, Vol. 1, "Essays on Planning and Economic Development," Warsaw, 1963.

73. ___, Wybor technik produkcji w krajach gospodarczo zacofanych. Panstwowe wydawnictwo ekonomiczne, Warsaw, 1963.

74. Farooquee, Q. N., Small-Scale and Cottage Industries as a Means of Providing Better Opportunities for Labour in India, Aligarh, 1958.

75. Fei, John C. H., and Ranis, G., "Innovation, Capital Accumulation and Economic Development," Yale University Economic Growth Center, No. 22, New Haven, Connecticut, 1963.

76. Galenson, W., and Leibenstein, H., "Investment Criteria, Productivity and Economic Development," The Quarterly Journal of Economics, August 1955.

77. Ganguly, A. K., "Economics of Small-Scale Industries. More Credit Required: Raw Material Shortage Hampers Expansion," A Survey of Indian Industries..., Calcutta, 1961, Capital, Supplement of June 29, 1961.

78. Garzouzi, E., Old Ills and New Remedies in Egypt, Cairo, 1957.

79. Gothoskar, S. P., "Report on the Survey of Cottage Metal Industry in Maharashtra State," Quarterly Bulletin of Economics and Statistics, Bombay, Vol. 1, No. 4, January-March.

80. "Government Attaches Great Importance to the Development of Small Industries," Pakistan Trade, Karachi, Vol. 12, No. 2, 1961.

81. "Growth Models for Illustrating the Effects of Alternative Employment and Investment Policies," Economic Bulletin for Asia and the Far East, Bangkok, Vol. 9, No. 1, June 1958.

82. Grunwald, K., and Ronall, J. O., Industrialization in the Middle East, New York, 1960.

83. Gupta, K. C., Small-Scale Industries, Delhi, 1962.

84. Handloom. Weaving Industry in India with Special Reference to Madras State, New Delhi, 1960.

85. Hont, E., "Home Economics in an Under-

108

developed Land," News Bulletin, New York, Vol. 28, No. 2, November 1952.

86. "Household Industry in 1961 Census," Economic Weekly, Bombay, August 19, 1961, Vol. 13, No. 33.

87. Jain, C. B., "Bid to Wipe Out Backwardness," Yojana, New Delhi, Vol. 6, No. 15, August 1962.

88. Jain, R. K., "Small-Scale Industry in Indian Economic Development," Modern Review, Calcutta, Vol. 112, No. 6, December 1962.

89. Joshi, N. J., "Whither Small-Scale Sector?", The Banker, New Delhi, Vol. 9, No. 10, December 1962.

90. Kahn, A. E., "Investment Criteria in Development Programs," The Quarterly Journal of Economics, Cambridge, Vol. LXV, No. 1, February 1951.

91. Kapande, S. V., "Development of Industrial Estates in Rajasthan," The Banker, New Delhi, Vol. 9, No. 5, July 1962.

92. Lakdawala, D. T., and Sandesara, J. C., Small Industry in a Big City. A Survey in Bombay, Bombay, 1960.

93. "Large Corporations and Economic Growth," Commerce and Industry, New Delhi, Vol. 55, No. 4, January 1961.

94. Mathai, P. M., "Rural Industries," Indian Worker, New Delhi, Vol. 10, No. 44-45, August 1962.

95. Menon, G. R. B., Value Economics, Calcutta-New Delhi, 1960.

96. "Mills Versus Powerlooms," Commerce, Bombay, Vol. 102, No. 2603, February 25, 1961.

97. Nanjappa, K. L. A., "New Method for Small Industries Development in Backward Areas, Journal of Industry and Trade, New Delhi, Vol. 11, No. 1, 1961.

98. Nanjundan, S., Economic Research for Small Industry Development, Bombay, 1962.

99. Parameshwaran, K. P., "Organization and Financing of Industrial Co-operatives," All India Co-operative Review, New Delhi, Vol.

28, No. 7, October 1962.

100. Parikh, G. O., "Rural Industries and Economic Growth," Indian Worker, New Delhi, Vol. 9, No. 28-29, April 17, 1961.

101. Ramakrishna, K. T. Finances for Small-Scale Industry in India, Bombay, 1962.

102. Ranganadha, S., "Handloom Weavers Unemployment and Elasticity Concept," AICC Economic Review, New Delhi, Vol. 13, No. 3, June 22, 1961.

103. Rao, M. V., "The Small and the Large," Yojana, New Delhi, Vol. 6, No. 15, August 5, 1962.

104. "Reorientation of Small Industries," Karachi Commerce, Vol. 13, No. 29-30, August 15, 1961.

105. Ryan, F. A., Efficiency for Small Manufactures, Bombay, 1962.

106. Sen, A. K., Choice of Techniques. An Aspect of the Theory of Planned Economic Development, Oxford, 1960.

107. Sahni, P. N., "Increase in Output," Yojana, New Delhi, Vol. 6, No. 15, August 5, 1962.

108. Sharma, S. L., "Extension Service," Yojana, New Delhi, Vol. 6, No. 15, August 5, 1962.

109. Shetty, M. C., Small-Scale and Household Industries, Bombay, 1963.

110. Shrimali, P. D., "Small-Scale Cottage and Village Industries," AICC Economic Review, New Delhi, Vol. 14, No. 10, 1962.

111. Singh, B., The Economics of Small-Scale Industries. A Case Study of Small-Scale Industrial Establishments of Moradabad, Bombay, 1961.

112. Tjan Ping Tjwan, "Population, Unemployment and Economic Development," Ekonomi dan Keuangan Indonesia, Djakarta, No. 9-10, tahun-ke 13, 1960.

113. Weddel, K., Aiding Small Industries Through Government Purchases, California, 1960.